How to Cook in High Heels

How to Cook in High Heels

SASHA PARKER   KORIN NOLAN

First published in Great Britain
in 2010 by
Absolute Press
Scarborough House
29 James Street West
Bath BA1 2BT
Phone 44 (0) 1225 316013
Fax 44 (0) 1225 445836
E-mail info@absolutepress.co.uk
Website www.absolutepress.co.uk

Publisher Jon Croft
Commissioning Editor Meg Avent
Art Director Matt Inwood
Design Matt Inwood and
Claire Siggery
Photographer Mike Cooper
Food Styling Genevieve Taylor
Style editor Laura James
Food editor Andrea O'Connor

ISBN 13: 9781906650377
Printed and bound by Jeming Srl, Italy

A note about the text
This book was set using Century, Modern No. 20 and
Greywolf Quirk typefaces. The first Century typeface was cut
in 1894. In 1975 an updated family of Century typefaces was
designed by Tony Stan for ITC. The Modern No.20 was first
issued by the Stephenson Blake foundry in 1905, designed in
the tradition of Victorian typography. The delightfully quirky
headline font, Greywolf Quirk font, is a contemporary font
designed by T. Jordan Peacock and can be found along with
his other designs at http://greywolf.critter.net/.

cONtENts

INtrODucTiON

This book is about food, fun, friends and family. It's about looking good and feeling great. It's about making life easy, without letting your standards slip and – importantly – it's a celebration of living life to the full.

We don't for a minute pretend to be professional chefs or beauty or lifestyle gurus. What we are is real women who like to eat delicious food, look as good as we can, live healthily, giggle with the girls, buy vertiginous heels and surround ourselves with those we love. And we want to do all of that without breaking the bank. After all, who can afford to spend a £1,000 on a pair of shoes or £500 on a face cream? Who has truffle oil in the cupboard or serves caviar to friends? Is all of this necessary to live a life that is both fun and glamorous? We don't think so.

How to Cook in High Heels is designed for real women everywhere. Whether you're a full-time mum or a workaholic, whether you spend hours in the kitchen each day or rarely set foot in, there really is something here for you.

We set out to show how easy it can be to put great food on the table every day and illustrate how each and every one of us has room for a little glamour in our lives.

It's amazing how many people say they can't cook and treat it as if it's a dark art. Cooking isn't rocket science and we've always felt that if you can read then you can cook. Which is why we set out to write a book designed to appeal to women just like us – busy mums juggling work, children and relationships and trying along the way to achieve some balance and have some fun.

Cooking for others feels, to us, like a selfish good deed. Sure, you're putting in the work creating something delicious for your friends or family, but you get so much back in seeing them enjoy the fruits of your labours.

Time in the kitchen should be soothing and restorative, not just another chore. That's why we've chosen to include recipes that are easy and achievable and cover off everything from feeding the kids through to hosting parties.

So, eat well, love life and be happy! Bon appetit...

WEEkDaY SuPPeRs

Life, for most of us at least, is high-pressure and faster than a speeding train. That's why it's really important to take time out for our partners, families, children and, of course, our friends.

How better to do this than round a table, enjoying good food, great conversation and perhaps a glass of wine or two?

Just because it's a miserable Monday or a wet Wednesday and the day's been long and hard, there's no need to fall into the trap of sacrificing wellbeing and glamour for a fast-food quick fix in an old T-shirt and a pair of sagging tracksuit bottoms.

When you've had an exhausting day working hard or looking after small children, it can be all too easy to flop in front of the TV with a takeaway or a microwaved ready meal. It might seem easy at the time, but it's good for neither the waistline nor the soul.

Instead, put on those favourite heels and a flirty little dress and grab a wooden spoon. We promise you'll be pleased you did. A short time spent in the kitchen will yield great results and everyone will thank you for it. Plus, eating real food, properly cooked, will offer a long-term mood boost and ensure you stay super-sexy.

Too often supper time is the only part of the day that families get to spend together, so it's important to ensure you eat together as often as you can. Chatting over supper, catching up on the day's events and giggling at someone's silly joke brings back lots of happy childhood memories for both of us.

And we think it's vitally important for kids to get that sense of a united family, whatever shape that family happens to be. Sharing food and conversation can go a long way towards bringing together a blended family and offers single and working parents some great one-to-one time with their kids.

We understand that life's a juggling act and – as mums ourselves – we know only too well how tricky it can be to please everyone. We also know how difficult it can be to get motivated after a long, hard day.

That's why we've taken care to include plenty of wholesome favourites here that everyone's sure to enjoy. Some of them are super-healthy, some a bit more indulgent, but all of them are really easy to make and delicious to eat.

So, go on give them a go...

fisH and MiXed Potato CHunky Chips

Who doesn't love fish and chips – it's a national institution. Eaten on a beach during the last days of summer, with half a bottle of champagne and a gorgeous man, there's nothing better. But be warned – when you buy from a chippie, you're looking at serious calories. Make this saintly version at home and while it's cooking you can polish your halo. There's not a frying pan in sight and the sweet potato is full of goodness. It's fish and chips with a twist – cutely retro and good enough for a dinner party.

Serves 4

4 large white potatoes (Maris Piper or King Edward are ideal), cut into large chunky chips
2 large sweet potatoes, cut into large chunky chips
2–3 tablespoons olive oil
salt
4 fresh fillets of cod or haddock, skinned
3 slices of slightly stale bread, blitzed into breadcrumbs in a food processor
4 tablespoons low-fat mayonnaise
2–3 tablespoons flat-leaf parsley, finely chopped
freshly ground black pepper
1 tablespoon low-fat margarine or butter
1 lemon, cut into large wedges

Preheat the oven to 180°C/Gas 5.

Place the white potato wedges in a baking tray, drizzle with one tablespoon of the olive oil and a little salt, then toss to coat thoroughly. Bake in the oven for about 25–30 minutes. Coat the sweet potato wedges with the remaining oil and salt. Add to the tray with the white potato wedges after about 20 minutes and leave to finish cooking.

Meanwhile, wash the fish fillets under cold water, pat dry with kitchen paper, then place on a lightly-oiled baking tray. In a bowl, mix together the breadcrumbs, mayonnaise, parsley, pepper and butter until combined. Mould this mixture evenly on top of each fillet of fish. Bake in the oven for about 15 minutes, or until golden brown.

Serve the fish with the mixed potato chips, lemon wedges and a sprinkle of fresh parsley.

Storecupboard staples

If you make sure you always have stocks of the basics, you'll be able to make a meal in minutes, never be without a snack and you won't be tempted to ring for a takeaway...

Olive oil
Great for everyday cooking, salad dressings and useful as an emergency moisturiser.

Sea salt and black pepper
Useful for pretty much every dish you'll need to cook.

Heinz tomato ketchup
You can pretend it's for the kids, but we know the truth!

Dried pasta
If you can, buy an Italian brand – after all, they're the experts. A selection of shapes is good, so try to keep in spaghetti, tagliatelli and penne.

Cheese
Parmesan for pasta, Cheddar for sandwiches and anything else that takes your fancy.

Tinned tomatoes
No one ever starved with a tin of tomatoes in the cupboard.

Tomato purée
An essential for delicious sauces.

Plain and self-raising flour
For sauces or whipping up a cake.

Rice
Arborio for risottos and rice pudding, Thai, jasmine or basmati for curries.

Icing sugar
For dusting and making fairy cakes with the children.

Stock cubes
Simply a God-send!

Mustard
Beef feels naked without it.

Garlic
Buy a string and hang it up in the kitchen.

Spaghetti Bolognaise

Channel your Italian goddess and whip up something delicious and hearty. If you're feeding a man, he'll love you for it and if you have a bambino or two, they won't notice the vegetables you've cunningly hidden.

We use turkey mince, rather than beef, because it's lower in fat and calories, and we go easy on the portion size. After all, a girl's got to watch her figure if she wants to squeeze into that little black dress.

Serves 4

1/2 onion, finely chopped
1 large carrot, peeled and finely chopped
1 celery stick, finely chopped
100g button mushrooms
2 garlic cloves, finely chopped
2 tablespoons olive oil
500g turkey mince
2 tablespoons tomato ketchup
1 x 400g tin chopped tomatoes
1/2 glass red wine
3–4 tablespoons Worcestershire sauce
1 teaspoon dried oregano
salt and freshly ground black pepper
400–500g spaghetti
3–4 tablespoons Parmesan cheese, finely grated
3–4 tablespoons flat-leaf parsley, finely chopped

Into a frying pan, add the olive oil followed by the chopped onion, carrot, celery, mushrooms and garlic and fry over a medium heat for about 5–10 minutes until soft. Add the mince to the pan and fry until brown, about 3–4 minutes.

Next, add the tomato ketchup, tinned tomatoes, red wine, Worcestershire sauce and oregano, mix thoroughly, then leave to simmer for 15–20 minutes. Season well.

Meanwhile, in a saucepan heat some salted water until boiling then add the spaghetti and cook according to the packet instructions until *al dente*. Strain and place the spaghetti on a plate with a few spoons of the turkey Bolognaise sauce on top. Sprinkle with the Parmesan cheese, the freshly chopped parsley and serve.

How to Cook in High Heels

EASY FISH PIE

Quick and simple to make, this is full of good things and tastes heavenly. Substituting starchy high-carb potatoes for celeriac ensures it's light enough to eat late and it's a great way to introduce a new vegetable to the children.

Serves 4–5

For the parsley sauce
2 tablespoons butter
1 tablespoon cornflour
200ml semi-skimmed milk
20g flat-leaf parsley, finely chopped

For the topping
500–600g celeriac or 6 medium Yukon Gold or Russet potatoes, peeled and chopped
2 medium parsnips, peeled and chopped
1 tablespoon butter
20g Cheddar cheese, grated
salt and freshly ground black pepper, to taste

500g mixed fish, deboned and chopped into large pieces (you can include salmon, cod, monkfish or whatever you fancy)
100g frozen peas
100g frozen sweetcorn (use tinned if you cannot find any frozen)

Preheat the oven to 180°C /Gas 5.

First, make your parsley sauce. Heat a saucepan over a low-medium heat and melt one tablespoon of butter. Add the cornflour and a dash of milk to create a paste (this is to avoid the cornflour going lumpy). Stir the paste for a minute or two to allow the flour to 'cook out'. Once the paste is smooth, add the rest of the milk and butter, heating gently to allow the butter to melt (you may need to use a whisk to thoroughly combine the paste). Once combined, stir continuously with a wooden spoon until the sauce begins to thicken; you may need to increase the heat slightly. Once the sauce has thickened, take it off the heat, add the chopped parsley and stir.

Next, steam the celeriac (or potato pieces) in a steamer for about 15 minutes or until just soft. Once cooked, remove and place in a large bowl. Add the butter, salt and pepper and mash thoroughly until smooth.

In a separate bowl, mix the parsley sauce with the fish pieces, frozen peas and sweetcorn to make the filling. Combine thoroughly then pour into the base of a baking dish. Dollop the mash on top of the fish mixture, spread out evenly with a fork and bake in the oven for 20–25 minutes until the fish is cooked and the top is starting to brown. Remove from the oven and sprinkle some of the grated cheese over the mash and season. Place back in the oven to bake for a further 10 minutes, or until the cheese is golden brown. Serve with steamed green vegetables such as sprouting broccoli or mange tout.

Korin's Cheat Thai Chicken Curry

I love the aromatic flavours of a Thai curry, which are lighter than the Indian version. This healthier – but no less delicious – recipe has all the taste you'd expect, but none of the fat, salt and colouring that you find in most curry house versions. We've used a ready-made Thai curry paste (it's quicker and cheaper) but, if you don't want to cheat, have time on your hands or are out to impress, we've included the recipe so you can make your own. But bear in mind that this dish is pretty spicy, so probably best not to cook it if you plan to do some serious smooching.

Serves 4

For the paste
3 shallots, peeled
3 cloves garlic
3 medium red chillies (remove the seeds if you want the paste to be milder)
$2^1/_2$cm cube ginger, peeled
juice of 2 limes
1 teaspoon Thai fish sauce
1 teaspoon ground cumin
1 teaspoon ground coriander
1 lemongrass stalk, roughly chopped
1 teaspoon freshly ground black pepper

For the curry
400–500g chicken breasts and/or thighs, skinned and diced
2 tablespoons olive oil
4 tablespoons your homemade curry paste or good-quality red Thai curry paste
$1/_2$ red pepper, sliced
125g shiitake mushrooms, sliced
100g green beans, chopped
1 x 400ml can reduced-fat coconut milk
6–8 baby sweetcorn, sliced
250g Thai fragrant basmati rice
4 tablespoons coriander, finely chopped
1 lime, cut into wedges

First, make the curry paste. Into a food processor add all the ingredients and blitz until you have a smooth paste.

Into a saucepan add the oil over a medium heat. Add the chicken pieces and fry until just starting to brown, then add the curry paste and mix thoroughly for 2–3 minutes so that it coats and seals the meat.

Next, add all the vegetables except for the sweetcorn and mix into the curry, cooking for a further 5 minutes or so. Add the coconut milk, mixing well to combine all the ingredients and leave for a further 5–10 minutes to simmer until the green beans are soft but still have a slight crunch. Then add the sweetcorn and cook for 2–3 minutes more.

Meanwhile, cook the rice according to the packet instructions. Strain and divide the rice between four plates before topping each with a good portion of the curry. Sprinkle with the freshly chopped coriander and serve with the lime wedges.

Seafood Lasagne

Lasagne gets a lot of bad press for being full of fat, but this version is filling enough to please your man (the mussels give it a surprisingly meaty texture), calorie conscious enough to keep your slinkiest friends happy and children will love the cheesy topping. If that weren't enough, it's also a mean hangover cure.

Serves 4–6

1 large white onion, finely chopped
2 cloves garlic, finely chopped, or
    1 teaspoon of garlic paste
1 tablespoon olive oil
2 x 400g tins chopped tomatoes
2 teaspoons caster sugar
1 teaspoon dried oregano
150g low-fat cream cheese
salt and freshly ground black pepper
650g mixed seafood such as prawns,
    mussels, squid and haddock
1 tablespoon cornflour
300ml semi-skimmed milk
100g mature Cheddar cheese, grated
8–10 dried lasagne sheets
handful fresh flat-leaf parsley, chopped

Preheat the oven to 170C / Gas 4.

Heat a saucepan over a medium heat and add the olive oil. Add the chopped onion and garlic and fry for 4–5 minutes until soft. Next, add the tinned tomatoes, sugar and oregano, mix well and leave to simmer for 2–3 minutes. Add the cream cheese, mix until thoroughly combined and season well. Then remove from the heat and mix in the seafood.

Into another saucepan, add the cornflour and a little of the milk to make a paste. Mix until thoroughly combined, then pour in the rest of the milk. Place the saucepan over a medium heat and stir continuously until the sauce starts to thicken, being careful to avoid lumps. (If it's looking a little lumpy, use a whisk to stir quickly for a few minutes to break up any lumps.) Then, add half of the grated Cheddar cheese and stir until the cheese has completely melted and the sauce has thickened. Remove from the heat.

Into a baking dish, place a layer of the seafood mixture, then cover with a layer of lasagne sheets. Repeat this process until you have used all the seafood mixture, being sure to end with a layer of lasagne sheets. Pour the cheese sauce over the top.

Place in the oven and bake for about 30 minutes. Half way through the cooking time, sprinkle over the remaining cheese and the chopped fresh parsley. Once the cheese has browned slightly, remove from the oven and allow to cool for 10 minutes before serving with a fresh green salad.

SOUPS

Soups offer a great way to get your five a day, are easy to make, perfectly consoling when you're tired or feeling low and – if you make more than you need – you can freeze what's left over to use when you're too busy or too tired to cook from scratch...

CaRRot and Ginger SouP

This soup is light and fresh and is as perfect for lunch as it is for a light supper. Use organic carrots if you can as they add so much more flavour.

Serves 4–6

1 large white onion, finely chopped
3 celery sticks, finely chopped
1.25kg organic carrots, peeled and
   chopped into small chunks
2 tablespoons olive oil
1.2 litres chicken stock
2¹/₂–5cm chunk of fresh ginger, peeled
salt and freshly ground black pepper,
   to taste

Heat a deep saucepan over a medium heat with a little olive oil, add the onions and celery and fry until just starting to brown. Add the carrots, stir, then cover with a lid and allow to simmer gently on a low heat, stirring every few minutes to avoid the vegetables sticking to the pan.

Once the vegetables are tender – this should take about 5–10 minutes – add the chicken stock and grate the ginger into the soup. Leave to simmer on a low heat for a further 15 minutes, uncovered, then turn the heat off and allow to cool a little.

Carefully, using a hand blender or a food processor, blend the soup for a few minutes until smooth. You may need to add a little more chicken stock if the soup is too thick. Season well with salt and pepper and serve with crusty brown bread.

How to Cook in High Heels

Quickies

Quick and tasty ideas to ensure supper is on the table in under 10 minutes.

Posh cheese on toast
Throw some Cheddar and stilton on to a piece of artisan bread and pop it under the grill until it's brown. Meanwhile, toss some salad leaves in a dressing and add some chopped tomatoes. Perfect served with olive jam.

Perfect scrambled eggs
Not just for breakfast, they make a perfect late supper too. Whisk up some eggs, add a splash of milk and some salt and freshly ground pepper. Melt a little butter in a pan and when it bubbles, add the eggs then let them sit for about 30 seconds before worrying them gently with a wooden spoon. Keep stirring until they're done. Top with smoked salmon if you want a romantic twist.

Brie and bacon focaccia
Fry some bacon in a pan. Meanwhile, slice some brie and split the focaccia. Place the brie on one slice of the bread and add the bacon when it's done. Pop the second focaccia slice on top and pop it in a toasted sandwich maker or under the grill until the cheese melts.

Simple pasta
If you're tired and hungry, why not cook some pasta, toss it in some olive oil, chop up some sun-blush tomatoes, a few basil leaves and sprinkle over lots of grated Parmesan and a grind of black pepper. No fuss and it's really consoling.

Chicken PASTA Soup

Substantial enough to be a meal in its own right, this soup is chunky, toothsome and full of natural goodness and it will satisfy even the hungriest man. Plus, it's so delicious that you'll have him eating out of your hand!

Serves 4–6

5–6 chicken thighs
1 large white onion, sliced
1 tablespoon olive oil
4 medium carrots, chopped into
    small dice
6–8 closed cup mushrooms, quartered
1/2 red pepper, seeds removed and
    chopped into small dice
1 x 400g can chopped tomatoes
600ml chicken stock
175ml white wine
100g frozen sweetcorn (use tinned if
    you cannot find any frozen)
salt and freshly ground black pepper
150g pasta shells
a handful of fresh coriander, chopped

Preheat the oven at 190°C /Gas 6.

Place the chicken thighs on a baking tray and roast in the oven for about 30–40 minutes, until cooked. Remove from the oven and leave to cool. Once cooled, remove the skin and separate the meat from the bones before cutting the meat into pieces.

Heat the oil in a deep saucepan over a medium heat, add the onions and fry for a minute or two before adding the carrots. Cook until the carrots and onions start to soften, about 5 minutes, then add the mushrooms and red pepper. Mix thoroughly and continue to cook until the mushrooms have shrunk in size and begin to brown.

Next, add the can of tomatoes, chicken stock, wine, sweetcorn and chicken pieces and season well with salt and pepper. Leave to simmer on a low heat, covered, for about 20 minutes.

Add the pasta to the soup and leave to simmer for a further 15 minutes or until the pasta is cooked, stirring occasionally to avoid the pasta sticking to the pan. Once ready, remove from the heat and set aside for half an hour, covered, to allow the flavours to infuse. When you're ready to serve, reheat the soup, pour into bowls and garnish with a sprinkle of fresh coriander.

Weekday wardrobe

Life can be frantic enough without having a clothes crisis. Ensure this never happens by stocking your wardrobe with these basics...

Crisp white cotton shirt
Perfect dressed down with jeans or dressed up with a gorgeous skirt. And tied at the waist and worn over a little dress, it can get you through the in-between months.

Two good pairs of jeans
One blue, one white. Find a cut that suits you and stick to that brand.

Good leather belt
Buy a good one and it will give any outfit a pulled-together look and will last for years.

Versatile jacket
The trick is to buy one that is smart enough for work, but also looks good with jeans and as a smart cover-up on chilly evenings.

Little black dress
It's a cliché, we know, but it really will take you anywhere.

Little white dress
As above, but for the summer.

Emergency glamour dress
You need this so you can be ready for last-minute dates or fab invitations that are sprung on you.

Fabulous underwear
It doesn't matter if no one sees it, you'll feel amazing wearing it and, if you have a man in your life, wear it for him and he'll be yours forever!

Signature scent
It can take a bit of finding, but 'the one' is out there and once you've found it, you can wear it forever.

Shoes
See our shoe menu on page 28.

Roast Sweet Potato, Parsnip and Bacon Soup

This has to be one of our favourite soups of all time. By roasting the sweet potato and parsnip it gives the soup added flavour and the smokey bacon is just the icing on the cake! The best thing of all, is that it's just so simple to prepare. Vegetarians could leave out the bacon and you would still have a delicious soup.

Serves 4

3 medium to large sweet potatoes, pricked all over
3 large parsnips, peeled and halved with the ends discarded
1 tablespoon olive oil
180g smoked bacon lardons (you can use smoked bacon rashers cut into pieces if you can't find lardons)
1 litre chicken stock
salt and freshly ground black pepper
1 tablespoon single cream (optional)

Preheat the oven to 190°C /Gas 6.

Place the sweet potatoes on a baking tray and roast them in the oven for about 45 minutes to an hour or until they are soft in the middle when pierced with a knife. The cooking time will depend on the size of the potatoes. For larger potatoes, you may need to leave in the oven for a bit longer.

Coat the parsnip pieces in the olive oil and lay them on another baking tray. Roast in the oven for about 30 minutes, or until the parsnips are soft in the middle when pierced with a knife.

Meanwhile, heat a deep saucepan over a medium heat and fry the lardons until brown. You will not need to add any oil before frying as there is enough fat in the lardons. Remove the saucepan from the heat to prevent the bacon burning while you prepare your other ingredients.

Once the parsnips are cooked, add these to the saucepan. Scoop out the cooked flesh of the potatoes and add this to the saucepan along with a little of the chicken stock. Return the saucepan to a low heat and, using a hand blender, begin to blend all the ingredients together, continuing to add the chicken stock gradually until you have a smooth consistency.

Add all the remaining stock, mix together thoroughly and season well with salt and pepper. Cook on the hob for about 10 minutes over a low to medium heat to allow all the flavours to infuse.

Serve with an indulgent drizzle of cream if desired and some crusty seeded bread.

SWEET TREATS

While it would be over the top to have a three-course meal every night, we think it's rather nice to have the odd pudding. And just because something is sweet, it doesn't have to be that sinful. Over the next few pages are a few great ideas for something slightly naughty, very nice and very easy.

LoW-FaT LeMOn and BeRRy CHEEsecake

Love cheesecake, hate calories? So do we. Which is why we're sharing our secret recipe for this guilt-free, heavenly pudding. You can have your cake and eat it and ensure you keep your figure too.

Serves 8

For the cheesecake
500g amaretti biscuits, crushed
2 egg whites
500g quark cheese
200g icing sugar
rind of 1 lemon
6–8 fresh mint leaves, to garnish

For the coulis
100ml water
225g raspberries, blueberries or
   strawberries, reserving some of each
   to use as a garnish
50g icing sugar

Preheat the oven to 170°C /Gas 4.

In a bowl, mix together the egg whites and crushed biscuits then press the mixture into a spring-form tin lined with greaseproof paper. (If you want a nice smooth edge, cut a circle of greaseproof paper to line the base, and a strip of greaseproof paper to line the sides of the tin.) Bake in the oven for about 15 minutes. Remove from the oven and place in the fridge to cool. If you want to cool it quickly, place in the freezer instead.

In a bowl, mix the quark cheese, icing sugar and lemon rind and combine thoroughly. Taste, and add a little more icing sugar if required to sweeten the mixture.

Remove the cake tin from the fridge (or freezer), dollop the quark mixture on top of the cooled biscuit base and spread out evenly with a spatula or palette knife. Place in the fridge for about an hour to chill. If you're in a rush, pop it in the freezer for

15–30 minutes to make sure it sets quickly.

While the cheesecake is chilling, make the coulis. Place a saucepan over a low heat, add the fruit and icing sugar and mix together well. Add the water to the fruit and simmer gently on a low heat for about 5 minutes until the fruit is soft and letting go of its juices. Taste the coulis, adding more icing sugar if you want it sweeter. Remove from the heat, allow to cool slightly, then blend the fruit with an electric hand blender. Allow to cool in the fridge until needed.

Once the cheesecake has chilled, carefully remove from the cake tin and place on a serving plate. Decorate with some of the fresh berries and mint leaves.

Serve a slice of the cheesecake with a drizzle of coulis over the top. If you have any leftover coulis, refrigerate it in a sealed container and serve over ice cream for a delicious quick dessert.

Meringues with Chocolate and Peanut Butter Sauce

Serve these for pudding and you'll be seen as a kitchen goddess. Bask in the glory but don't, for a second, be tempted to count the calories.

Serve 4

For the meringues
4 medium organic egg whites
200g caster sugar

For the sauce
100g dark chocolate, minimum 70%
  cocoa solids
1 teaspoon butter
1 tablespoon golden syrup
1¹/₂ heaped tablespoons crunchy
  peanut butter
4 large scoops good-quality vanilla
  ice cream

It took us a little while to perfect our meringues if we are completely honest....they are one of those recipes that are so easy to make if you follow the instructions to a tee!

First of all it is imperative that you have a clean bowl without any traces of grease lurking on the sides. Secondly, you must ensure that you don't let any egg yolk get into your egg whites and, finally, stick to the recommended whisking time (yes, you will need to time yourself) to get your peaks especially glossy and away you go!

Preheat the oven to 140°C /Gas 1. Separate the egg whites into a clean, dry bowl (one at a time into a separate bowl before pouring them into the main big bowl – this way, if a little yolk should creep through it won't spoil the other whites!) Start whisking with an electric whisk until you create soft peaks; this should take about 2 minutes. (Apparently it can be done by hand, but we attempted it once and not only did our arms nearly drop off, but it takes a good half-hour if not more to get them right and even then we didn't!)

Once the egg whites are soft and fluffy, gradually add the sugar whilst continuing to whisk. Once all the sugar has been added, continue to whisk on a high speed for 7–8 minutes (here's the bit where you need the timer) until you have beautiful glossy peaks.

Line a baking sheet with baking parchment, dabbing a little of the meringue mixture underneath on the corners to stick it down. Spoon the meringue mixture onto the sheet to make 4 large individual meringues, moulding with the back of a spoon or spatula to create a little well in the middle (big enough to fit a nice ball of ice cream!). Place in the middle of the oven to bake for 1 hour exactly. Once the meringues are cooked, remove from the oven and leave to cool completely.

To make the sauce, heat a pan of water over a high heat until boiling. Break the chocolate into pieces and combine with the butter in a heatproof glass bowl. Place the bowl over the pan of boiling water and stir until the chocolate and butter have almost melted. Add the golden syrup and peanut butter and continue to stir for a further minute, until the syrup and peanut butter have dissolved. Remove from the heat.

To serve, place a large dollop of ice cream in the middle of each meringue and drizzle with the chocolate and peanut butter sauce.

Shoe Menu

Chocolaty Orange Brownies

Who can resist chocolate? Not us, that's for sure and these brownies are heaven in a tin. They prove that a Terry's Chocolate Orange is not just for Christmas and will have everyone coming back for seconds.

Serves 10–12

185g dark chocolate, minimum 70% cocoa solids
185g butter, cubed
3 large eggs
275g golden caster sugar
85g plain flour
40g cocoa powder
100g Terry's Chocolate Orange, broken into small pieces (you can use a mixture of white, dark and milk chocolate orange)

Pre heat the oven to 160°C /Gas 4.

First, line the bottom of a 20cm square baking tray with baking parchment, putting a little butter underneath the corners of the sheet to help stick it down. Into a heatproof glass bowl, add the pieces of dark chocolate and the butter and place over a pan of gently simmering water, being careful to ensure the bowl doesn't touch the water. Stir occasionally until the chocolate and butter have melted. Remove from the heat.

Meanwhile, using a high-powered whisk, whisk together the eggs and sugar in a bowl until the mixture has doubled in size and is very thick and frothy. This will take about 5 minutes or more, so stick with it!

Next, spoon the chocolate mixture into the egg mixture and very slowly fold together using a metal spoon, being careful to fold instead of mixing as this will knock out all the air you have created in the whisking stage. Once the chocolate and egg mixture is thoroughly combined, sieve in the flour and cocoa powder and repeat the folding process until it is just combined, but don't over-mix. Towards the end of this process, mix in the chocolate orange pieces.

Pour the mixture into the baking tray, spreading out evenly with a spatula and bake in the oven for around 30 minutes, making sure you don't open the door before the first 25 minutes. After 30 minutes, check the consistency by gently shaking the baking tray; if it wobbles quite a bit, place it back in the oven for a further 5–10 minutes until cooked. The surface should be shiny and glossy. Remove from the oven and leave to cool completely in its tray before turning out and cutting into big chunks to serve.

Balancing Acts

As working mums we know a thing or two about juggling and have had to work hard to achieve a real balance in our lives. We don't pretend to have all the answers, but here are a few tips that have kept us sane...

Accept that there aren't enough hours in the day and that all we can do is our best in the time we have. Once we realised this, life got a lot less stressful.

Ditch the idea that you can have everything, all of the time. It's a myth and will only lead to huge disappointment. Rather than fretting about achieving the impossible, focus on really appreciating what you have and spend time doing lovely things.

No one has the perfect life. It's easy to look at Hollywood stars and tabloid babes and imagine there's nothing wrong in their lives. This, though, is invariably untrue.

Accept that if you're a working mother some things have to give. You might have to miss something your child is involved in but, as long as you're honest about why you have to work and make it up to them afterwards, they should understand. Speak to your child and find out what's really important to them – you might think they're desperate for you to attend sports day, but for them it might not matter a jot.

We're passionate about work – it's a huge part of who we are and it's a driving force in our lives. But we also realise that not everyone feels the same way. For some of us, work is simply about making enough money to pay the bills and put food on the table. Whichever camp you fall into, you must remember that we all need to take time out. It's unlikely that without you someone will die or the company will collapse and everyone works better after a rest.

Indentifying priorities and being super organised will put you on the right path to achieving a balance. Show us someone who successfully juggles their life and we'll show you a list maker. Lists focus us and are motivating as we can see what we've achieved at the end of the day.

We're notebook obsessed. Having a notebook full of useful contact numbers and information you need to have to hand definitely saves time and avoids the frustration of not being able to find out something you really need to know.

If you're a working mother, then you'll know good childcare is key to keeping you sane. It's always the way that the one time your babysitter lets you down, you'll absolutely have to be somewhere momentously important. So it makes sense to have a back-up plan. Making friends with other mums is key here as you can help each other out of a crisis.

Set aside time for the important things in life – time with your children, partner, family and friends. Make arrangements, write them in your diary and stick to them. It gives everyone something to look forward to.

Make a date night with your man. It's crazy, but it's all too easy to become ships that pass in the night and then to wonder where it all went wrong when the divorce papers land on your doorstep. Take action early and, 10 years into the relationship, you'll be as happy as the day you met. Take turns to choose what to do. It can be as simple as a candlelit supper at home or a trip to the movies. It's the time that's important, more than what you do with it.

Finally, remember that all work and no play will make you a very dull girl! We may not have the energy or inclination to party hard every night, but having fun social events to look forward to – even if it's just a dinner party at home – makes life that little bit more exciting. We all know that spending time chatting and laughing with friends makes us feel fabulous, so make sure you do it as often as you can!

BODY & SOUL

What we eat has a real effect on how we look and feel.

Choose the wrong food and you'll feel lethargic and depressed, you'll pile on the pounds and your skin will suffer. Choose the right foods and you'll have bags of energy, your skin will glow, your hair will shine and all will seem well in the world.

When we're feeling tired or in need of a boost, it's easy to reach for a bar of chocolate or to order a takeaway. But quick-fix foods leave us feeling worse in the long run. What we really need is something soothing, clean and restorative, such as the dishes we've included here.

Health and beauty go hand in hand and the best way to look good is to take real care of yourself. The beauty industry is worth millions and it's easy to fall into the trap of forking out for the latest miracle cream. But your kitchen cupboards might well yield something just as good. That's why we've included some foodie facemasks guaranteed to leave you looking radiant.

There's nothing better than waking up in the morning feeling energised and raring to go. A good diet, lots of water and plenty of sleep will ensure you feel this way every day.

It pays to start the way you mean to go on, so ensure you have a really good breakfast. If you don't you'll find your good intentions fail by mid-morning and you'll be tucking into a bar of chocolate.

The good news is that eating healthily needn't be dull or difficult as the quick and easy recipes here show. Try them and you'll be surprised how good you feel....

Roasted Salmon and Sweet Potato Salad

A brilliant mood booster, this makes a great lunch or light supper which will support you through a busy or stressful time. Salmon is a great source of Omega-3, sweet potatoes are rich in complex carbohydrates and this dish is packed full of feelgood vitamins. It tastes great, too, so what's not to love?

Serves 2

1 large white onion, finely sliced
2–4 vine tomatoes, finely sliced
2 medium-sized salmon fillets, skinned and boned
2 tablespoons soy sauce or balsamic vinegar
salt and freshly ground black pepper
300g sweet potato, cubed
3–4 tablespoons olive oil
200g mixed lettuce leaves
1 red pepper, seeds removed and sliced
1 large avocado, peeled, stone removed and sliced
250g mozzarella, or a handful of baby mozzarella balls, torn into pieces

Preheat the oven at 200°C /Gas 7.

To prepare the salmon fillets, place on a sheet of foil, then layer with the sliced onions and tomatoes. Pour over the soy sauce (or balsamic vinegar) and season well with salt and pepper. Wrap the fish up tightly in the foil – you may find it easier to use two layers of foil to seal the fish properly – and bake in the oven for 25 minutes.

Meanwhile, place the sweet potato pieces on a baking tray and coat with a little oil and salt. Bake in the oven for 20–25 minutes, being sure to keep an eye on them. Turn them once or twice during the cooking time to make sure they cook evenly.

To make the salad, arrange the lettuce, sliced peppers, avocado and torn mozzarella on a large serving plate. Once the salmon and sweet potatoes are ready, arrange on top of the salad, roughly breaking up the fish into bite-sized pieces. Drizzle with a little olive oil and enjoy.

Glow girl!

We know it can be hard to get healthy, but a little effort and some small changes can make a big difference...

Always take the stairs instead of the lift. It may be a slog at first, but you'll soon find yourself racing up them.

Set an alcohol limit – perhaps one glass of wine when you're at home and two on a night out.

Walk or cycle instead of taking the bus or driving. Not only is it good for you, but you get a different perspective on the world.

Join a team. Whether it's netball, hockey or even football, everyone's good at something. Plus, it's a great way to meet new people.

Do some exercise at home. Press-ups or sit-ups don't take much time, but do make a huge difference.

Don't yo-yo diet. It never works and can feel like hell. Once you fall into the habit of healthy eating, it's easy to stick to it. And if you fall off the wagon every now and then, don't think you've failed. Just climb back on again.

Teriyaki Salmon with Brown Rice and Pak Choi

This is the foodie equivalent of a yoga work out or time spent meditating. It's soothing, restorative and as good for the body as it is for the soul. Brown rice has more vitamins, minerals and fibre than its white counterpart and the pak choi is great for digestion. It's also delicious, so you can feel smug as you savour every mouthful.

Serves 4

For the teriyaki sauce
40g brown sugar
1 teaspoon garlic powder
1/2 teaspoon ground ginger
4 tablespoons tomato ketchup
60ml soy sauce
40ml cider vinegar
10ml Worcestershire sauce

4 medium fresh salmon fillets, skinned and boned
16 vine-ripened tomatoes
1/2 onion, finely chopped
2 pak choi, each sliced in half lengthways
240g brown organic short grain rice

Pre heat the oven to 190°C /Gas 6.

First, make your teriyaki sauce. Combine all the ingredients for the sauce in a bowl and mix thoroughly until smooth. Set aside. (If you have any sauce left over, store in a sealed container or jar in the fridge.)

Place each salmon fillet onto a separate sheet of foil and then fold the edges of the foil up around the fish to create a 'boat' shape, being sure to scrunch the foil tightly so that no juice will escape. Place these on a baking tray.

Next, scatter 4–5 tomatoes on top of each salmon fillet and sprinkle over the chopped onion. Then spoon 4–5 tablespoons of the teriyaki sauce over each salmon fillet and carefully bring the foil together to seal the fillet, making sure you squeeze the foil tightly. Bake in the oven for 25 minutes.

Meanwhile, cook your pak choi. Bring a saucepan of water to the boil and blanch the pak choi for a couple of minutes only. Once blanched, remove from the water, heat a frying pan on a medium-high heat with a little olive oil and fry the pak choi for a couple of minutes on each side, turning once.

Bring a saucepan of water to the boil (or use the blanching water from the pak choi) and cook the rice according to the instructions on the packet.

Once the fish is cooked, remove from the foil and serve with brown rice and half a pak choi. Drizzle over the delicious juices from the salmon and enjoy!

How to Cook in High Heels

TuNa AsParagus RisoTTo

Seriously yummy, the ingredients in this dish are packed full of vitamins and goodness designed to leave you feeling full of energy.

Serves 4

100g asparagus, woody ends removed
5 tablespoons butter
2 garlic cloves, finely chopped
1 teaspoon olive oil
salt and freshly ground black pepper
1 large white onion, finely chopped
350g of Arborio rice
$1/2$ cup of dry white wine
4 medium tuna steaks or 400g tinned
    tuna in brine
zest of 1 lemon
50g Parmesan cheese, grated
small handful of parsley, finely chopped

Bring a saucepan of water (about 1 litre) to the boil and blanch the asparagus for 1–2 minutes. Remove from the boiling water and immediately submerge in cold water. Retain the asparagus cooking water and place to one side. Cut the asparagus spears into even pieces.

Heat a saucepan over a medium heat with two tablespoons of butter. Once the butter is foaming, fry the chopped garlic, add the asparagus pieces, one tablespoon of water, some salt, pepper and olive oil and fry until tender. Tip into a bowl and leave to one side. Add another two tablespoons of butter to the saucepan and add the chopped onion. Fry over a medium heat for 2–3 minutes until starting to soften, then add the rice and stir well for 1–2 minutes, ensuring that the rice is thoroughly combined with the butter and onion.

Next, add the wine to the saucepan and reduce almost completely. Then add enough asparagus water to cover the rice by 1cm. Bring to a simmer and stir once.

Once the rice has absorbed nearly all the water, add some more asparagus water to cover the rice by 1cm, again, stirring once. Repeat this process adding the water gradually until the rice is soft but still *al dente*. (Note: you may not need to use all the asparagus water, so be sure to

taste your rice as you're cooking to make sure you do not overcook it.)

If you are using fresh tuna steaks, season the tuna with salt and pepper while the rice is cooking. Place a frying pan over a medium heat, add a tablespoon of oil and cook the tuna steaks for about 6 minutes, turning once half way through. Remove from the pan and break the tuna into flakes. Place to one side. If you are using tinned tuna, drain thoroughly.

Once the rice is cooked – this should take about 25–30 minutes, turn the heat off and add the asparagus pieces, one tablespoon of butter, the lemon zest, tuna flakes and a generous amount of Parmesan cheese and stir well. (This is where you would also add your canned tuna, if you don't use tuna steaks.)

Serve immediately with a good sprinkle of Parmesan and chopped parsley. Buon appetito!

Garlic Spinach Chicken

with Spicy WEDGES and Salsa

For the chicken

4 teaspoons butter, softened
3 teaspoons garlic paste
small handful of parsley, finely chopped
4 chicken breasts, skinned
salt and freshly ground black pepper
150g fresh spinach
100ml chicken stock
1 small onion, finely sliced
16 baby tomatoes on the vine, sliced

For the wedges

550g white potatoes, cut into wedges
   (Maris Piper or King Edward ideal)
salt and freshly ground black pepper
1 teaspoon paprika
1 teaspoon chilli powder
4 tablespoons olive oil

For the salsa

1 small red onion, finely chopped
2 medium/large tomatoes, finely
   chopped
1/4 cucumber, finely chopped
1/2 red pepper, finely chopped
1 medium avocado, peeled and finely
   chopped
juice of 1/2 lemon
2 tablespoons flat-leaf parsley, finely
   chopped
garlic oil, to drizzle (if you don't have
   garlic oil, use good quality olive oil)
salt and freshly ground black pepper

This dish is designed to give you an energy boost. Chicken is rich in protein and spinach has high levels of tryptophan, an essential amino acid. The spicy wedges and salsa add a real kick, making this a mood-boosting must if you're feeling weary.

Serves 4

Preheat the oven at 190°C /Gas 6.

In a bowl mix together the butter, garlic paste and parsley. Slice the chicken breasts lengthways without cutting right through and fill each cavity with a large teaspoon of the garlic butter, then close them up again. Season well with salt and pepper.

Lay a 'bed' of fresh spinach in the bottom of a baking dish, then pour the chicken stock over the spinach. Place the chicken breasts on top of the spinach, covering each one with the sliced onion and tomatoes, then season well again. Cover the baking dish with foil and place in the oven to bake for 30 minutes.

Meanwhile, prepare your wedges by placing them in a baking tray and drizzling with olive oil. In a small bowl, mix the salt, pepper, paprika and chilli powder together, then sprinkle over the wedges with another drizzle of olive oil. Bake the wedges in the oven for 30–40 minutes, or until they are golden brown.

While the wedges are baking, make your salsa by mixing together all the ingredients, season well with salt and pepper and drizzle with the garlic oil or good quality olive oil.

To serve, place the chicken and spinach alongside some of the crispy wedges and serve a good dollop of the fresh salsa on the side of the plate.

How to Cook in High Heels

TUrkey and PineaPPle SwEEt and SoUR

Turkey is a low-fat meat high in protein and pineapple is said to sharpen the memory. So this dish offers the perfect combination to keep you sharp and switched on.

Serves 4

For the sweet and sour sauce
2 tablespoons cornflour
100ml water
4 tablespoons soft brown sugar
4 tablespoons soy sauce
6 tablespoons white wine vinegar
2 tablespoons tomato ketchup

For the turkey
1–2 tablespoons olive oil
450g turkey breast, diced
1 red pepper, seeds removed and cut into chunks
1 green pepper, seeds removed and cut into chunks
1 bunch spring onions, chopped into large pieces
100g baby sweetcorn, sliced down the middle
100g pineapple chunks (you can use tinned but be sure to drain well)
240g brown organic basmati rice, to serve

First, make your sweet and sour sauce. Into a small pan, add the cornflour and a little bit of water to form a paste. Place the pan over a low heat and cook gently for 1–2 minutes, then add the rest of the sauce ingredients, mix together well and stir continuously with a wooden spoon until the sauce has thickened. Remove from the heat and set aside.

Next, heat a frying pan over a medium heat and add a little oil. Fry the turkey pieces for about 7 minutes, or until the turkey begins to brown. Add the pepper and spring onions to the pan and pour the sauce over the top of the turkey. Mix well to coat all the ingredients and continue to cook for another 5 minutes.

Once the peppers begin to soften a little, add the sweetcorn and the pineapple chunks and cook for a further 5 minutes.

Meanwhile, bring another saucepan of water to the boil and cook the rice according to the packet instructions.

Serve the turkey over the rice with plenty of sauce.

Heavenly housework

Housework doesn't only leave your home looking lovely – it can have a great effect on your figure too. Take a look at how many calories you burn doing everyday jobs for just 30 minutes

Half an hour cooking something will burn a whopping 90 calories

Never again complain about washing up as you'll burn around 80 calories

Getting back to nature and doing a spot of gardening comes in at 160 calories burned

General housework, such as dusting, polishing and tidying, will lose you around 130 calories

Dashing away with the smoothing iron will get your shirts crisp and your figure trim as you'll be burning 80 calories

Sweeping the floors will see you clear away around 90 calories.

CHiCKen PaD THai

We were told by a girl we met while filming, that this was the best Pad Thai she'd ever tasted – not bad considering she'd been travelling in Thailand for three months. While Pad Thai might not usually be considered healthy, our version is packed full of fresh vegetables and contains shiitake mushrooms, which are said to boost the immune system. We've used roast chicken here as it tastes amazing and uses up leftovers, but you can use fresh chicken breasts if you prefer.

Serves 4

2–3 tablespoons Thai 7-spice
2 tablespoons runny honey
4 tablespoons olive oil
1/2 medium/large roasted chicken, skinned, boned and chopped or torn into small pieces
1 red pepper, seeds removed and finely sliced
1 bunch spring onions, finely sliced
165g shiitake mushrooms, sliced
100g mange tout
150g unsalted peanuts, crushed
2 packets Pad Thai ready-to-wok noodles (if you prefer the dried variety, be sure to cook according to the packet instructions first)
6 limes
3–4 tablespoons Thai fish sauce
200g bean sprouts
2 eggs, beaten
a small bunch fresh coriander, roughly chopped

In a bowl mix together the Thai 7-spice, honey and oil to form a paste. Add the chicken and mix well, ensuring that the chicken is thoroughly coated in the marinade. Set aside, covered, and leave for as long as you can, but at least one hour, to allow the flavours to infuse. (It can be used straight away if you don't have time to let it marinate.)

Once the chicken has marinated, heat a wok over a medium heat and add a little oil. Add the chicken and fry for 2–3 minutes, stirring continuously. Then add all the vegetables apart from the beansprouts and continue to fry for a further few minutes, being sure to keep stirring to avoid any chicken or vegetables sticking to the wok.

Meanwhile, heat a non-stick frying pan over a medium heat and gently toast the peanuts for a few minutes. Keep them moving to make sure they don't burn – you just want to brown them lightly. Remove from the heat and leave to one side.

Add the noodles to the wok, breaking them up as you go, then squeeze in the juice of 2 limes and the fish sauce. Keep stirring to avoid sticking! Add the bean sprouts and cook for a further few minutes.

Heat another frying pan over a medium heat with a little oil and add the eggs, scramble for a few minutes until just cooked, then transfer them straight to the wok and combine with the other ingredients.

Pile the Pad Thai onto a large serving dish, sprinkle with the toasted peanuts and coriander and garnish with the remaining lime, cut into wedges. Serve immediately.

How to Cook in High Heels

Skin-Purifying Salmon Pie

Salmon is an excellent source of Omega-3 essential fatty acids, which are important for healthy skin, hair and nails. Sweet potatoes are high in fibre and spinach is cleansing. This really is virtue on a plate!

Makes 2 small individual pies

2 sweet potatoes, peeled and cubed
2 tablespoons olive oil
$1/_2$ medium-sized onion, finely chopped
2 cloves garlic, finely chopped
200g chopped tinned tomatoes
4–5 basil leaves
a big handful fresh spinach leaves
1 large salmon fillet, skinned and sliced into even pieces
25g butter
salt and freshly ground black pepper, to taste

First, place the sweet potatoes in a steamer and steam until soft, about 5–7 minutes, then set aside.

Meanwhile, heat a non-stick frying pan over a medium heat and lightly fry the onion and garlic in the olive oil until soft. Add the chopped tomatoes, basil leaves, and spinach and cook for 3–4 minutes until the spinach has wilted.

Place the salmon pieces evenly in the bottom of two individual pie dishes. Pour over the tomato and spinach sauce, leaving enough room for a layer of mashed potato on the top.

In a small bowl, mash the sweet potatoes with the butter, salt and pepper, then dollop into the pie dishes over the tomato sauce. Smooth the mash out evenly, then place the pie dishes in the oven to cook for about 20–25 minutes, until the potato is starting to brown.

Serve with steamed greens such as asparagus or green beans.

Get your beauty sleep

Sleep is vitally important. It allows your body to recharge and heal itself. Most healthy adults need around eight hours of sleep per night. But it's not always easy to get to or to stay asleep. Try these tips...

Get some exercise. Even 20 minutes of gentle walking can decrease the stress hormones that interfere with sleep.

Don't eat a heavy meal late at night. If you do you could end up tossing and turning for hours and may well get indigestion too.

Go to bed and get up at the same time every day. Sure, there'll be times when you want to stay out late and party hard and that's fine as long as you usually stick to the routine.

Sex is a good sleep aid, so it's a perfect excuse to get snuggly with your man.

Get rid of the electronic fog in your bedroom. Even the tiniest of lights, such as those of mobile phones or TVs on standby, can seriously interfere with sleep.

Set an electronic curfew. Don't watch TV or use a computer for an hour before bedtime. Instead, use the time to wind down. Go for a walk, have a warm bath, read a book or do some gentle stretches instead.

Kitchen cupboard beauty treats

The bathroom cabinet isn't the only place to store your beauty fixes and pick-me-ups. The kitchen storecupboard can be every bit as useful...

One of our favourite beauty concoctions is a brown sugar and olive oil scrub. It smells divine and is a brilliant exfoliator, particularly for drier areas such as knees, elbows and feet. You need to use three times as much sugar as olive oil and mix them together. Use just as you would a shop-bought exfoliator before a bath or shower and you'll end up with baby-soft skin.

A honey face mask is brilliant for getting rid of impurities as honey is a natural antibiotic. Simply smooth whatever honey you have to hand over your face and lie back and relax for 10 minutes before rinsing it off with warm water.

Oatmeal is a great beauty treat; simply mix some with water and a squeeze of lemon juice and you have a brilliantly effective facial scrub. You can allow it to dry as a mask, too, if your skin is in need of a little more care. Then wash it off with warm water, while gently exfoliating as you do so.

Cucumber & Avocado Beauty Dip with Crudites

This is perfect if you're looking to detox, but also makes a great everyday snack or light lunch. Packed full of good stuff – including avocados, which contain monounsaturated fat, which has a positive effect on cholesterol levels – and half an avocado counts as one of your five-a-day.

Serves 2–3

1 ripe avocado, peeled and halved
$1/3$ of a cucumber, peeled and grated
2 heaped tablespoons low-fat bio yoghurt
juice of $1/2$ lemon
cayenne pepper, to taste

To make the dip, place the avocado in a bowl and mash well, then add the grated cucumber. Add the rest of the ingredients and mix together well.

Transfer the dip to a serving bowl and serve with an assortment of chopped crudités such as sliced red pepper, carrot sticks, or steamed asparagus or broccoli.

Kedgeree

Traditionally this dish can be quite heavy on fat, with lots of butter and cream. We've made ours more saintly, by adding some seafood which gives it a nice twist. Fish and eggs are both high in Omega-3 and protein and brown rice is seriously good for you.

Serves 4

1 onion, finely chopped
1 tablespoon olive oil
1¹/₂ tablespoons of hot curry paste
400ml full-fat or semi-skimmed milk
400ml cold water
320g boneless mixed fish pieces, including cod, salmon and smoked haddock (you can buy these in a fish pie mix pack)
240g brown basmati rice
150g frozen peas
6–8 scallops, shelled and cleaned thoroughly
140g prawns, pre-cooked and shelled
2–3 tablespoons fresh coriander, finely chopped
2 lemons, cut into wedges
4 poached or boiled eggs, to serve

Heat a frying pan with the olive oil and fry the onion over a medium heat for a few minutes until soft. Add the curry paste and mix well, cooking for a further few minutes until the spices release their fragrance. Remove from the heat.

Into a saucepan, add the milk and water and bring to a simmer. Then add the mixed fish pieces, reduce to a low-medium heat, then leave to poach for about 3 minutes before turning the heat off. (The fish will finish cooking while sitting in the hot milk.)

Return the frying pan containing the onions to the heat, add the rice and mix well. Gradually add the milk/water to the rice, pouring in just a little at a time so that the liquid just covers the rice (similar to cooking a risotto). Once it has been almost completely absorbed, add some more liquid, stirring a few times to combine with the rice. Continue to add the milk/water to the rice until it is almost cooked. (You may not need all the liquid, or you may need to add a little more water). It's a good idea to taste the rice as you go along to see how much more liquid it will need to finish cooking.

Next, add the peas and continue stirring the rice so that it doesn't stick to the bottom. Heat a separate frying pan and add a little oil. Place the scallops in the pan and fry for a couple of minutes each side. Depending on how big they are you may need to cook them for an extra minute on each side, but be careful not to overcook them. Remove from the pan and leave to one side.

Add the prawns to the rice and keep mixing until the prawns are thoroughly heated through. When the rice is cooked and all the liquid is absorbed transfer the kedgeree onto a large serving plate and top with the fish and scallops. Sprinkle with the chopped coriander and a poached or boiled egg and garnish with the lemon wedges alongside.

The power of pilates

We're both big fans of pilates and Korin is a qualified instructor. Here are a few reasons why it's our workout of choice...

Pilates both changes and benefits your body, creating long, lean and toned muscles as opposed to short bulky ones.

The slow, controlled movements of pilates target the deepest abdominal and core muscles which many other techniques overlook.

Pilates teaches awareness of the breath and alignment of the spine.

Pilates aims to elongate, strengthen and restore the body to balance.

It can benefit pretty much everyone, regardless of their age and fitness level.

Visit famouslyfit.com and check out Korin's pilates column.

Mixed Mushroom and Spinach Quinoa Risotto

We're huge fans of quinoa and believe that everyone should try to include it in their diet at least once a week. This grain is unusually rich in amino acids, as well as magnesium and vitamin E. Mushrooms are high in selenium, which is an antioxidant, which, together with vitamin E, helps to protect cells from the damaging effect of free radicals. If you're a really good girl, you can leave out the wine and replace it with more stock.

Serves 4–5

1 onion, finely chopped
3 cloves garlic, finely chopped
2 tablespoons olive oil
175g quinoa
700ml chicken stock
200ml white wine
600g mixed mushrooms including
  oyster, shiitake and chestnut, sliced
100g fresh spinach leaves
2–3 tablespoons low-fat crème fraîche
salt and freshly ground black pepper
a small handful of chopped flat-leaf
  parsley, to serve
50–100g Parmesan cheese, grated

Heat a frying pan over a medium heat and lightly fry the chopped onion and garlic in a little olive oil until soft. Add the quinoa and mix well to coat with the onion mixture.

Next, add all the stock, stir and allow to cook for a few minutes before adding the wine and the mushrooms. Reduce the heat and leave to simmer gently for 20–25 minutes until almost all of the liquid has reduced and the quinoa is cooked.

Stir in the spinach leaves and allow them to wilt completely, then remove from the heat and stir in the crème fraîche. Season well and leave to stand for a few minutes before serving.

Serve with a sprinkling of fresh parsley and Parmesan cheese.

PancaKes

Good news, girls – pancakes can be healthy. These two takes are so delicious, you'll never reach for the chocolate spread again! Everyone loves them, even the kids. Blueberries are packed full of antioxidants, walnuts are high in Omega-3 and bananas are high in potassium. Pancakes that are good for us. Have we discovered the Holy Grail?

Makes about 10 small American-style pancakes

Wholemeal Blueberry Pancakes

50g butter
200g wholemeal self-raising flour
1 teaspoon baking powder
1 large free-range egg
300ml full-fat milk (or you can use semi-skimmed if you're health-conscious)
225g fresh blueberries

to serve
crème fraîche
maple syrup

Wholemeal Banana & Walnut Pancakes

50g butter
200g wholemeal self-raising flour, sieved
1 teaspoon baking powder
1 egg
400ml full-fat milk (or you can use semi-skimmed if you're health-conscious)
2 medium-sized bananas, peeled and mashed
100g walnuts, crushed

to serve
crème fraîche
maple syrup

To make the pancakes, begin by melting the butter in the microwave or in a saucepan on the stovetop. Into a large mixing bowl place the flour and baking powder, then add the egg, milk and melted butter. Whisk all the ingredients together (you can do this with an electric whisk if you like) to make a smooth batter.

Depending on which pancakes you are making, stir in either the blueberries or the mashed banana and walnut pieces.

Heat a large frying pan over a medium heat and add a little butter or spray oil.

Dollop large spoonfuls of the pancake batter into the pan. (You will probably have room for about 3 small pancakes.)

Once the pancakes have cooked on one side (about 3–4 minutes) you will see small bubbles appear on the surface. Flip the pancakes over with a spatula and cook the other side for a further 3–4 minutes. The pancakes should have risen and be golden brown when ready.

To serve, pile 3 or 4 pancakes on a plate topped with a huge dollop of crème fraîche and lashings of maple syrup.

How to Cook in High Heels

Very BeRRy and BraZil DeTox BreAKfast

Start the day as you mean to go on with this blissful breakfast. Lemon cleanses the body, raspberries are packed with antioxidants, bio-yoghurt is great for digestion – encouraging the good bacteria and fighting the bad – and Brazil nuts are high in selenium and zinc.

Serves 2

1 cooking or Granny Smith apple, peeled and roughly chopped
50–100g fresh raspberries
juice of 1/2 lemon
2 tablespoons honey
2 heaped tablespoons low–fat natural bio yoghurt
100g Brazil nuts, finely chopped

Into a saucepan place the chopped apple and raspberries. Add two tablespoons of water and stew on a low heat until soft, stirring occasionally. Add the lemon juice and honey to the fruit and mix together well. Remove from the heat and pour into a serving dish. Cover, and leave in the fridge to cool (this is best done the night before and left overnight in the fridge to cool completely).

To serve, dollop the yoghurt on top of the cooled fruit and sprinkle with the chopped Brazil nuts. You may also wish to add a little extra honey to sweeten.

Sunflower Seed, Apricot and Raisin Flapjacks

Life is all about balance and, while we're not for a moment saying that flapjacks are as healthy as raw carrots or spinach leaves, we think that eating a little of what you fancy is a good thing. And, as lots of healthy ingredients have made their way into our flapjacks, you can feel a tiny bit virtuous. Better a small helping of this than a bag of crisps or a bar of chocolate.

Makes 10–12 squares

180g butter
100g golden caster sugar
4 tablespoons golden syrup
1 tablespoon honey (optional, or can be replaced with another tablespoon of golden syrup if you prefer)
275g soft rolled oats
100g ready-to-eat dried apricots, finely chopped
100g raisins
50g sunflower seeds

Preheat the oven to 180°C /Gas 6.

Heat a saucepan over a medium heat and add the butter, sugar, golden syrup and honey (if using). Stir until well combined and completely melted. Remove from the heat.

In a large mixing bowl, combine all the other ingredients, add the syrup mixture and mix together well.

Line the bottom of a baking dish with baking parchment and lightly grease the sides with butter. Pour in the flapjack mixture and spread out evenly, pressing the mixture down firmly into the dish with the back of a spoon.

Bake in the oven for 20 minutes. You may need to cover the dish with foil half way through if the flapjack is starting to brown too much on top.

After 20 minutes, remove from the oven and leave to cool completely before turning out onto a board and cutting into squares – the ideal lunchbox treat!

SmootHieS

Not just for summer, smoothies make a great start to the day. They provide at least one of your five-a-day, and are brilliant instead of a snack when you feel your energy flagging. But just in case you were starting to think we are too good to be true, we've included a tip on how to add a sinful twist to these smoothies should you be in a party mood.

Jamaican Touch

Bring all the flavours of the Caribbean to your kitchen with this delicious drink. Perfect for the garden when the sun is high and the music is pumping.

Serves 2 (adult-sized glasses)

juice of 2 oranges
1 banana, peeled
1 teaspoon caster sugar
1 tablespoon water
240ml pure orange juice
approximately 10 large ice cubes

Place all the ingredients into a blender and whizz until combined.

Sinful? Just add rum.

Bittersweet Pleasure

While the lime makes this smoothie quite tangy, this mixture of fruits is really refreshing and satisfying. A truly mouthwatering combination...

Makes 2 large glasses

1 eating apple, peeled, cored and cut
  into chunks
50ml pure apple juice
2 kiwi fruit, cut in half with the flesh
  scooped out
juice of 1 lime
approximately 10 large ice cubes

Place all the ingredients into a blender and whizz until combined.

To make this drink sweeter, just add a cup of pure apple juice or a teaspoon of granulated sugar.

Sinful? Just add Jack Daniels.

Tropical Teaser

Packed with tropical fruits, this smoothie will fuel a daydream. Just imagine you have your own little island, far away from the hustle and bustle of everyday life. Bliss...

Makes 4 large glasses

2 passion fruits, cut in half with the
  flesh scooped out
1/4 pineapple, cut into chunks
1 small mango, peeled and cut into
  chunks
1/2 litre pure orange juice
approximately 5 large ice cubes

Place all the ingredients into a blender and whizz until combined.

Sinful? Just add Malibu.

FaCE MaSKs

With simple, healthy and easy-to-find ingredients such as bananas, avocados, cucumbers and honey, these face masks are simple to prepare... and almost good enough to eat! They're designed to feed your skin and leave it looking radiant.

Banana and Honey Wrinkle-release Face Mask

Bananas are packed full of vitamins, including A and B, as well as folic acid which will moisturise and soften your skin, help prevent wrinkles and smooth the appearance of any you may already have. Honey has healing qualities and will help to repair and protect your skin. If you're skin is greasy, add a tablespoon of oats. These will absorb grease, remove impurities and gently exfoliate the skin.

Makes 1 mask

1 banana, peeled
1 tablespoon honey

In a small bowl, mash the banana to a pulp, add the honey and mix well. Gently smooth over the skin and leave for 20 minutes, then rinse off with tepid water.

Avocado, Honey and Olive Oil Mask for Dry Skin

Dry skin is uncomfortable and ageing, so it's important to keep your skin hydrated. Avocado is an excellent moisturiser and olive oil restores your natural glow, while the honey binds the mask, protects the skin and adds a delicious fragrance to this gorgeous face mask.

Makes 1 mask

1/2 ripe avocado, peeled and mashed
1 teaspoon olive oil
1 tablespoon honey

In a bowl, mix together all the ingredients to form a smooth paste (it's easier to do this with a hand blender or electric whisk). Smooth evenly over the skin, leave for 20–30 minutes before washing off with a warm damp flannel or towel and tepid water.

Aloe Vera Refresh and Hydrate Your Skin Mask

We all have days when our skin looks tired. This mask will have your skin back to normal in no time. The cucumber helps to clean and feed your skin, while the aloe vera will help to soften it. You'll be left feeling blissfully relaxed.

Makes enough for 2–3 masks

1/2 cucumber, peeled and cut into chunks
2 tablespoons oatmeal
2 tablespoons aloe vera gel (you can buy this in most pharmacies and supermarkets)
1 tablespoon cornflour (yes, really)

Using a blender or food processor, blend the cucumber and oatmeal together. Add the aloe vera gel and the cornflour and mix again, then transfer to a small bowl and place in the microwave for 1 minute on high to thicken, stirring after the first 20 seconds.

Transfer to the fridge to cool. Once cooled, the mixture should be a good spreadable texture that will hold and smooth evenly over your face. You can also cut up a few slices of cucumber for your eyes.

Leave on the skin for 20 minutes before rinsing off with tepid water.

an at-HOME PaMPer DaY

Wouldn't it be blissful to spend every morning at a spa or salon being polished to perfection? Sadly the real world doesn't allow for this. In reality most of us make do with some DIY treatments and the odd trip to a professional. But setting aside a day to pamper yourself can leave you looking and feeling amazing...

Begin the day with our Very Berry and Brazil Detox Breakfast (the recipe's on page 51) and a cup of green tea. Then go for a short walk or do some gentle stretches.

Once you're feeling relaxed, make a brown sugar and olive oil scrub. See page 42 for the recipe.

Next apply a face mask. Take a look at the page opposite for our recipes and choose the one most appropriate to your skin type. Apply the mask and lie back, listening to some soothing music.

Remember this day is all about relaxing. So avoid quickly checking your emails or catching up on a bit of work. Avoid switching on the TV too. Instead, read a book or get out into the garden to plant some herbs or do some weeding. This will leave you feeling grounded.

A light lunch is next on the agenda. Try our Cucumber and Avocado Beauty Dip with Crudités (see page 42) or Mixed Mushroom and Spinach Quinoa Risotto (see page 46).

After lunch give yourself a pedicure. Remove any old polish and then soak your feet in a bowl of water. Add a couple of drops of an essential oil or bath oil of your choice. Clip or cut your nails straight and then to make sure they're smooth. Push back the cuticles using an orange stick wrapped in cotton wool or the tool designed for it. Remove any hard skin with a foot file. Separate your toes with a tissue, foam separator or pedicure sandals if you have them. Apply a base coat and let it dry. Apply two coats of polish and leave it at least 10 minutes to dry. Then add a top coat. Allow your nails a good 90 minutes to dry.

Mid-afternoon mix up a delicious smoothie (see page 54 for suggestions) and get some serious relaxing in. Lie in the garden if the weather's nice or curl up with a good book if the rain's coming down in buckets.

Have an early supper that's soothing and restorative. Try our salmon pie on page 41. Then run yourself a rose-scented bath and have a long, indulgent soak.

Don't be lured into watching TV. Instead climb into bed early and read a book until you drop off.

a TASTe Of Us

They say you are what you eat and we think this is true in more ways than one. The food we enjoy, the way we cook and the way we approach kitchen life is often informed by our childhood experiences. Recipes are handed down through families and, with them, comes a connection to the past.

As times change and the world moves on, we're anchored by our history and cooking something our mothers made for us and serving it to our own children creates a wonderful continuity.

Family folklore is important in making us feel we belong, as is tradition, however ordinary. So, the roast beef your mother served each Sunday, the birthday cake that gave you months of delicious anticipation, or even the fish and chips you savoured every Friday night all go towards making up your culinary legacy.

If travel – or a culturally diverse family – feature in your background then you'll probably benefit from a rich culinary heritage.

Korin was born in Korea. Her family moved back to Sheffield when she was still just a baby, which remained her home until her teenage years, when she moved to France, before finally settling in London with her son Liam.

Sasha was born in Greenwich to an English mother and a Jamaican father. She was raised in south-east London before spending her teens travelling, eventually settling down in Kent with her girls, Bobbi and Eevy.

Our backgrounds have given us some great foodie experiences and have taught us a lot about the joy of diversity in the kitchen. We wanted to share some of the recipes we've stumbled upon on our journey through life, so here are some of our favourites...

a LiTTle bit abOUT Me...

I've been hugely influenced by the foods I encountered during my childhood and teens and my parents always encouraged me to be adventurous with food. They travelled a lot (I was born in Seoul in South Korea) and they would often cook dishes from the countries they had visited.

I've always loved food and developed a passion for baking early on. This may well have been a rebellion against my mother's penchant for healthy eating. While my friends were scoffing burgers and chips, my mum would be insisting we tucked into a lovingly prepared bean feast.

We almost always ate organic food and I did eventually become quite fond of tofu. When I was about six, my mother put a kiwi fruit in my lunchbox and it caused quite a stir at school. Everyone, including the dinner ladies, gathered round in amazement to see what it was. Well this was Sheffield in 1984!

When I was 16 we moved to France, where, just two years later, I had my son Liam, who is half French. I lived with my partner of the time's parents in the Dordogne for a few months. It was foodie heaven. They grew their own vegetables and there were cépes growing in a nearby forest.

There wasn't much to do in the Dordogne, except to cook, and I learned a great deal about French cooking using fresh local ingredients. French women have such a healthy attitude to food; they don't deprive themselves of anything and the foods they eat are often full in fat and high in calories. Yet, because they eat only small portions, they don't pile on the pounds.

The following recipes are just a taste of my culinary heritage and I hope you enjoy them as much as I do.

DANDE aux ABricots

In France my family became very close to a wonderful – and rather eccentric – English lady called Barbara. She lived with her French husband, Claude, and would often invite us for dinner. We used to hope that this would be the dish she served and often recreated it at home. It's ridiculously easy and tastes divine...

Serves 2–3

1 packet dried French onion soup or
*   1 tin of good quality French onion*
*   soup*
500ml white wine (you will need to
*   add another 250ml if using dried*
*   soup)*
400g tin of apricots
1 large free-range turkey leg

Preheat the oven to 175°C /Gas 4.

In a bowl, mix together the dried or tinned soup, wine and apricots. Place the turkey leg in a baking dish and pour over the soup mixture.

Place in the oven for around 2 hours basting the leg regularly with the sauce until it is cooked through and the meat starts to come away easily from the bones when prodded gently. After about 2 hours, the sauce will have reduced and become thick and sticky. Remove from the oven and allow to rest, covered, for at least 15 minutes.

Serve with roast potatoes or rice and lightly steamed green beans with the sauce drizzled over the top.

PoULet ROTi a la ProVEncale

In the Dordogne, life was quiet and I cooked a lot. My boyfriend's mother taught me about French country cooking and we would use the herbs and vegetables grown in the garden. This was one of the simplest dishes she taught me and one of the most delicious..

Serves 4–5

1 large free-range chicken (about 650–700g)
sea salt and freshly ground black pepper
1/2 lemon
1 large white onion, peeled and cut in half
1 sprig fresh rosemary
1 sprig fresh thyme
5 tablespoons butter, softened
3 cloves garlic, finely chopped
3–4 tablespoons flat-leaf parsley, finely chopped
260ml glasses white wine
Ratatouille, to serve (see page 62)

Preheat the oven to 200°C /Gas 7.

First, prepare the chicken. Sprinkle all over with salt and black pepper and rub gently into the chicken skin. Inside the chicken cavity, place the lemon half, one half of the onion, rosemary and thyme.

In a small bowl, mix half of the softened butter with the chopped garlic and parsley and stir well to combine.

Carefully lift the skin away from the chicken without breaking it and gently push a tablespoon of herb butter underneath between the skin and flesh, prodding it along so that there is one spoon of herb butter on either side of the bird's breastbone. Then rub the chicken all over using the remaining plain butter.

Chop the remaining onion half into quarters. Place the chicken in the centre of a roasting tray and scatter the onion quarters around it. Pour in the white wine and bake the chicken in the oven for 30 minutes. After 30 minutes, increase the heat to 220°C /Gas 8 for a further hour. (The cooking time will depend on how big your chicken is. You may need a little less or a little more cooking time.) During the cooking time, baste the chicken occasionally with the fat from the bottom of the tray. If you find that the chicken is browning too quickly on top, cover it with foil half way through.

To test if your chicken is cooked, prod the breast of the chicken with a metal skewer; the chicken is cooked when the juices run clear. Remove the chicken from the oven and set aside, covered with foil, to rest for 15 minutes before carving. Serve hot with a large dollop of the Ratatouille alongside.

How to Cook in High Heels

RaTatOUille

If possible, make this the night before as the flavours have time to meld overnight and when it's reheated the next day it'll taste delicious.

Serves 6–8

10 large organic vine tomatoes, peeled and cored
3 tablespoons olive oil
3 large white onions, cut into large chunks
6 cloves garlic, peeled and roughly chopped
2–3 mixed peppers (different colours), cut into chunks
herbs de Provence (fresh if possible, including basil, thyme and parsley)
140g tomato paste
2 aubergines, cut into medium chunks
5 courgettes, cut into medium chunks
salt
freshly ground black pepper

To peel the tomatoes, first cut an 'X' in their bases as this will make them easier to peel, then place them in a bowl and cover with boiling water. Leave for 2 minutes then drain in a colander. Once they are cool enough to handle, peel the skin off carefully (you might find this easier using the blunt edge of a knife). Then remove the core using an apple corer or a small knife.

Heat a deep saucepan over a medium heat with the olive oil and fry the onions, garlic and peppers for a few minutes until they begin to soften. Cover, reduce the heat to medium and cook for a further 20 minutes, stirring regularly to keep the vegetables from sticking. Add a little olive oil as necessary if they do start to stick.

Next, add the peeled tomatoes whole, the herbs de Provence and the tomato paste. Stir to combine well and cook for a further 15 minutes over a medium heat. Add the aubergine and courgette chunks to the ratatouille, reduce the heat to low and cook for a further 30 minutes until all the vegetables have softened. Season well with salt and pepper and serve with roast chicken.

How to Cook in High Heels

Beef and ALE Stew
with a HuGe YorkSHire PuDDing

As I come from Sheffield it would be a crime not to include Yorkshire pudding. Sunday lunch at home was unthinkable without it and I loved it best when we had it with Beef and Ale Stew. It's the perfect combination for a cold, lazy Sunday and is quick to prepare, although the stew needs to cook slowly for at least three hours..

Serves 2–3

For the stew
3 tablespoons olive oil
500g stewing steak, cut into cubes
1 large white onion, roughly chopped
2 large carrots, peeled and roughly chopped
4–5 celery sticks, roughly chopped
3 garlic cloves, peeled
600ml British pale ale
300ml strong beef stock
200g frozen peas (use tinned peas if you cannot find any frozen)
2–3 tablespoons flat-leaf parsley, finely chopped

For the Yorkshire pudding
150g plain flour
150ml semi-skimmed milk
100ml cold water
2 medium free-range eggs
a big pinch of salt
2–3 tablespoons olive oil

Preheat the oven to 220°C /Gas 8.

Into a deep saucepan add the oil and place over a medium heat. When the oil is hot, add the beef and sear quickly, stirring continuously for a few minutes until the meat is brown all over. Remove the meat from the pan and set to one side.

Add the chopped onion, carrots and celery to the pan and fry for 5 minutes, stirring occasionally to keep them from sticking. Return the meat to the pan, add the garlic cloves and pour in the ale, cooking for a further 2 minutes before adding the beef stock. Place a lid on the saucepan, reduce the heat to low and simmer for about 3 hours, stirring occasionally. During the last half an hour of cooking time stir in the peas and the parsley.

Meanwhile, make your Yorkshire pudding. In a large mixing bowl, combine the flour and salt and make a well in the middle. Pour in the water, milk and eggs and, using an electric hand whisk, whisk the ingredients until you have a smooth batter.

Pour about half an inch of oil into the bottom of a roasting tin (or medium sized tins if you are making individual puddings) for about 20–30 minutes, or until the oil is spitting hot. Remove from the oven very carefully and pour the mixture into the roasting tin(s) and return to the oven, turning the heat down to 180°C /Gas 5. Bake in the oven for 30 minutes until the puddings have fully risen.

Remove from the oven and serve the hot stew in the middle of the Yorkshire puddings.

Clafouti aux Cerises

This is a sort of French custard cake and is absolutely delicious. It also forms a huge part of my culinary heritage as it's my mum's absolute favourite thing to eat. So this one's for you Mummy...

Serves 8-10

100g self-raising flour
1.2 litres milk or cream
4 medium free-range eggs
200g caster sugar
2–3 teaspoons vanilla essence or a
  sachet of vanilla sugar
pinch of salt
500g very ripe black cherries, pitted
  (you can buy cans of pitted cherries
  if fresh cherries are not in season)

Preheat the oven to 175°C /Gas 4

In a large mixing bowl, combine all the ingredients except for the cherries and whisk together well.

Pour the mixture into a lightly-greased cake or flan tin and scatter the cherries over. Bake in the oven for about an hour until the clafoutis is set right through to the middle. (Test this by inserting a knife in the centre to see if it comes out clean. If it doesn't, you may need to cook the clafoutis for a further 5–10 minutes.

Leave to cool completely before serving.

Carrot, Apple and Lemon Drizzle Cake

When I was in my teens I was charged with baking cakes for my dad's weekend shiatsu courses. I'd get home from school on a Friday, pop my pinny on and get baking. I got quite good at improvising and using whatever was in the cupboard. This was then – and still is – one of my very favourite cakes...

Makes 10–12 slices

For the cake
200g caster sugar
100g butter
2 medium/large free-range eggs
300g self-raising flour
1 teaspoon baking powder
1 teaspoon allspice
3 small/medium carrots, peeled and
  grated
2 Granny Smith apples, peeled and
  chopped into small chunks

For the icing
150g icing sugar
juice of 1½ lemons

Preheat the oven to 170°C /Gas 4.

Lightly grease the sides of a loaf tin and line with baking parchment.

In a large mixing bowl, combine the sugar and butter and, using an electric whisk, beat until smooth. Once smooth, add one egg at a time, beating between each one until thoroughly combined.

Next, add the flour, baking powder and allspice to the bowl and whisk again until fully blended, then add the carrot and apple and stir together well.

Pour into the loaf tin and place on the middle shelf of the oven to bake for about 45 minutes. After the first 25 minutes of cooking time you may find you need to cover the cake with foil to prevent it from going too brown on top. To test if the cake is ready, insert a clean wooden skewer into the centre; if the batter is still gooey it will need another 10 minutes or so.

Remove from the oven and set aside to cool for half an hour, then transfer to a plate. The easiest way to do this is by holding a folded clean tea towel in one hand and flipping the cake onto it. Remove the tin and any baking parchment and replace with an upturned plate before carefully flipping the cake the right way up with the plate underneath.

In a small bowl, make your icing. Mix together the icing sugar and lemon juice until smooth (you may need to add a small dash of warm water if the icing is too thick), then pour the icing all over the cooled cake, allowing it to drip down the sides. You can do this while the cake is still warm.

Leave to cool completely before serving with a good cup of tea.

a LiTTle bit abOUT Me...

South-east London, where I grew up, was a bit of a culinary desert and, as a child, I was a horribly fussy eater. As I was made to eat everything on my plate, I vowed that as soon as I reached adulthood I would survive on a diet of only burgers and chips. I am now, of course, extremely glad I changed my mind.

I travelled in my teens, doing work experience, which included sheep herding in Iceland. Sheep's Head is one of the traditional dishes I found myself trying – proving, I think, that I'd grown out of my previous fussiness. At the ripe old age of 17 I ate my first – and last – sheep's eye. It was a bit

squelchy and the texture was extreme, but I did commit to a fair bit of chewing before deciding it wasn't for me. The experience did, however, open up a whole new landscape for me as I realised that I had nothing to lose by trying new foods.

I didn't really come into my own in the kitchen until I had my first daughter, Bobbi, when I was 18. I'd been lucky enough to eat in a few amazing restaurants and had begun to appreciate the different flavours, textures and combinations that were served. I decided early on that I wanted my daughter to experience great food from an early age.

Initially I wasn't a natural cook, but I discovered that great cooking is something that can be learned and practice really does make perfect. Once I fell in love with cooking it became apparent how truly easy it is to put good food on the table.

I've included here some Jamaican dishes I adore as well as a couple of my mum's favourites that warmed the cockles of my heart and melted in my mouth. Just remember, you don't need to be an amazing chef to produce delicious food. With the desire to eat well and the will to have a go you'll be dishing up yummy food in no time...

SaUSage MEat SURprise

My mum invented this dish when bored in the kitchen one day. I have no idea how it got its name, but we're sticking with it. It's a dream to make and even my girls, who object loudly whenever they see an onion or tomato, love it. So it's definitely a family favourite that spans the generations...

Serves 4

800g pork sausage meat
4 medium tomatoes, sliced
1 large white onion, sliced
1 large Granny Smith or cooking
   apple, cored, peeled and sliced
500ml ready-made gravy

Preheat the oven at 180° C/Gas 5.

Using half the sausage meat, line the base of a large baking tray being sure to spread it out evenly. Then lay the sliced tomatoes, onions and apple over the top of the sausage meat to form another layer. Spread over the remaining sausage meat in an even layer and place in the oven to bake for about 45 minutes.

Meanwhile, make your gravy according to the instructions on the packet.

Once the sausage meat surprise is cooked, carefully drain off any excess cooking juices from the bottom of the tin, reserving 2 tablespoons for the gravy.

Mix the reserved juices into the gravy. Serve the sausage meat surprise in slices with boiled new potatoes, lots of vegetables and lashings of gravy.

CuRRied ChiCKen

This is probably one of the easiest and most accessible Jamaican dishes. If you haven't had Jamaican food, then make this the first dish you try. The fusion of aromas and flavours demonstrates how amazing Jamaican food can be and will leave you wanting to try more...

Serves 4

4 chicken fillets, skinned and cut into
  small pieces
juice of 1 lime or lemon
2 tablespoons curry powder
1 garlic clove, crushed
1 large white onion, chopped
1/2 green pepper, seeds removed and
  finely chopped
1 teaspoon dried thyme
salt
freshly ground black pepper
3 tablespoons olive oil
240g basmati rice

Place the chicken pieces in a small bowl and add the lime (or lemon) juice. Mix together well to ensure the chicken is thoroughly coated. Drain off any remaining juice and then add the curry powder, chopped garlic and onion, green pepper, thyme, salt and black pepper. Set aside to marinate for about an hour. (If you don't have time, you can cook it straight away).

Heat a frying pan or wok over a medium heat with the olive oil, add the chicken and it's marinade and cook for 10–15 minutes, or until the chicken is completely cooked (you may need to cut a piece open to check).

Meanwhile, cook the rice according to the packet instructions. Drain and serve with a large spoonful of the chicken curry on top.

Jamaican Rum BrEAd PUDding

Really simple to make and even easier to eat, this dish will leave your kitchen awash with the warm, rustic Jamaican aromas of cinnamon, nutmeg and rum...

Serves 6

1 loaf of slightly stale white bread, sliced
225g caster sugar
3/4 teaspoon ground cinnamon
1/4 teaspoon ground nutmeg
225g butter, melted
150g raisins
3 tablespoons of Jamaican rum
225ml condensed milk
900ml full-fat milk
5 medium free-range eggs, beaten

Preheat the oven to 175°C /Gas 4.

Lightly grease a large square baking dish with butter and line it with baking parchment.

Cut the crusts off the bread and tear it into small pieces. Place the bread in a large mixing bowl and add the sugar, cinnamon, nutmeg, raisins, rum and melted butter. Mix together well before tipping into the baking dish.

Into a separate bowl, add the condensed milk, full-fat milk and eggs and beat to combine with a whisk. Pour over the bread mixture in the baking dish.

Bake in the oven for 1 1/4 hours. Check your pudding half way through the cooking time to make sure it isn't browning too quickly. If it is, cover it with tin foil. The pudding is cooked when a clean knife inserted in the centre comes out clean.

Serve a decent portion, warm, with good quality vanilla ice cream.

GranDad's EaSt End STew

This dish is a basic but delicious stew dreamed up by my amazing granddad, Steve Deacon. He passed the recipe down to my mother and then she taught me to make it. Eating it brings back memories of being at Nan's for a family get-together and then sitting down next to Granddad to eat. In his immortal words, 'Go on girl, tuck in'...

Serves 4

2 tablespoons olive oil
500g oxtail, cubed
2 large white onions, roughly
  chopped
1 large leek, sliced
1 large turnip, grated
2 large parsnips, peeled and sliced
4 large carrots, peeled and grated
2 heaped tablespoons pearl barley
2 heaped tablespoons red lentils
4 large Maris Piper potatoes, chopped
  into large chunks
2 litres beef stock

Heat a deep saucepan over a medium heat with the olive oil and fry the oxtail pieces quickly for a few minutes just to seal the meat, then add the onions and leeks and fry for about 5 minutes, until soft. Add enough beef stock to just cover the meat. Simmer on a low heat for about 40 minutes.

Next, add the turnips, parsnips, carrots and a little more beef stock (just enough to cover the vegetables). Reduce the heat to low and simmer again for about 15 minutes, until the vegetables begin to soften.

Add the chopped potatoes, pearl barley and lentils and simmer for a further 30 minutes. Stir the stew regularly to avoid the lentils sticking to the bottom.

To serve, ladle the hot stew into bowls and serve with fresh crusty bread.

KiDs in the KitCHen

When your children are tiny, it's very easy to feed them healthily. As they get a bit older, it becomes trickier. They're exposed to marketing messages on TV and pressure from their peers can lead them to behave in a certain way and often that involves junk food and fizzy drinks.

A great way to get your children to eat better is to get them involved in the cooking. If they're small they'll love spending time with you and will find it an adventure. As older children seem to spend so much time playing computer games and chatting online, something as simple as making muffins can seem, to them, so enchanting.

Nowadays there are all sorts of issues around food, with both obesity and eating disorders on the rise. These things are best fought at home and a balanced diet, with the odd treat, is the best way to set a child on the road to a healthy relationship with food. And it stands to reason the best place to learn about these things is in the kitchen at home.

Knowing how to cook is a real life skill that can make all the difference as children grow older. Their first tentative steps out into the world are much easier when they know the basics of how to look after themselves. Doing something well boosts confidence and they'll be hugely popular with their friends if they can whip up something delicious in the kitchen. And where better to explore new culinary landscapes than at home? Rainy days spent in the kitchen will be something they remember for the rest of their lives, so why not start them cooking right now…

Korin's EGGy BaSKEts

Korin used to make this fun little breakfast dish for her mum and dad each Sunday morning. Children are always attracted to novelty and the basket element provides just that. It's also the perfect vehicle to sneak in tomatoes, so even the fussiest of eaters won't notice.

Serves 4

4 slices thick wholemeal bread, crusts removed
2–3 tablespoons butter
2 tomatoes, cored and cut into chunks
6 medium free-range eggs, beaten
3–4 tablespoons water
salt and freshly ground black pepper
2 tablespoons flat-leaf parsley, chopped

Preheat the oven at 170°C /Gas 4.

First, butter each slice of bread on both sides. Fold the corners of each slice into the middle pressing down gently without breaking the bread. Place the slices on a baking tray and bake in the oven for 5–10 minutes, until the bread is golden brown and crispy. Remove from the oven and, while the baskets are still warm, gently ease open the corners a little then set aside.

In another small bowl combine the beaten eggs, water, salt and pepper and whisk together with a fork until frothy.

Heat a frying pan over a medium heat with a little olive oil and gently fry the tomato chunks for 1 minute, then add the egg mixture and continue to stir with a spatula until the eggs are scrambled and just cooked.

To serve, spoon the scrambled eggs into the middle of each basket, sharing the mixture out evenly, then sprinkle with a little of the chopped parsley.

How to Cook in High Heels

Tips to keep kids in the kitchen

As soon as supper's over, children want to race off to watch TV or play computer games, so keeping them chatting can be tricky. Try these games to stop them running off...

The never-ending story game
The first player starts with a word such as 'she'; the second may take up the story with 'went'; the third with 'to'; the fourth with 'the'; the fifth with 'zoo' and so on. The aim is not to let the story end and often it's hilarious seeing where imagination takes the group.

Scrabble with a theme
Pick a theme – such as food, clothes, or cars – and play a normal game of Scrabble. Anyone who comes up with a word related to the theme gets double points.

21 Dares
The first player begins counting from 1. You can say up to three numbers – for example, 1, 2 – and then the next person might say 3, 4, 5. Keep going until you get to 21. Whoever is left having to say 21 has to do a dare dreamed up by the group.

Spot the lie
This is huge fun with a big group of friends, as children love to learn things about adults. You get to learn a lot about each other. Someone round the table must make three personal statements, two true and one a lie. For example, I can speak Swahili, I once drove a racing car and I own 200 pairs of shoes. The group must then guess which of these is a lie.

LaMB MEatballs and SPAGhetti

Spaghetti offers children a free pass to get as messy as they like. But who are we to complain when we take into account the health benefits of this dish? Lamb is a good source of iron and is rich in zinc, so we're happy to mop up the spills.

Serves 4

For the meatballs
500g of lamb mince
1/4 onion, finely chopped
2 tablespoons flat-leaf parsley, finely chopped
200g plain flour
salt
freshly ground black pepper

For the sauce
1/2 onion, finely chopped
1 garlic clove, finely chopped
2 x 400g tins chopped tomatoes
2 tablespoons tomato ketchup
2–3 tablespoons Worcestershire sauce
1 teaspoon granulated sugar
1 1/2 tablespoons dried oregano
1–2 tablespoons olive oil
salt and freshly ground black pepper

400g spaghetti

First, make the meatballs. Into a mixing bowl place all the ingredients (except the flour) and combine well – it's easier to do this by hand. Form the mixture into balls (you will find this easier if you wet your hands a little), then lightly roll each meatball in the flour, shaking off any excess and place them on a plate. Set aside.

Heat a frying pan over a medium heat with a little olive oil and fry off the onions and garlic until soft. Add the tomatoes, Worcestershire sauce, sugar and oregano, mix well. Reduce the heat to low, cover, and allow to simmer for 10–15 minutes while you cook the meatballs.

Meanwhile, heat another frying pan with a little olive oil over a medium heat and fry the meatballs until browned all over and cooked all the way through, about 10–15 minutes. (You may have to check this by breaking one in half.)

Once cooked, add the meatballs and lamb juices from the frying pan into the tomato sauce and stir well. Turn the heat down very low and allow to simmer for a further 5 minutes.

Cook the spaghetti according to the instructions on the packet until *al dente*. To serve, dollop spoonfuls of the meatballs and sauce over the top of the pasta and garnish with a good sprinkle of the chopped fresh parsley.

How to Cook in High Heels

FiSH CakES

It can be tricky to get kids to eat fish, but not with these little beauties. Children love to help and can get stuck in shaping the mixture into patties. Sometimes we serve them in a burger bun with salad and ketchup. For an added kick for grown-ups, add a little Thai green curry paste to the mix.

Makes 6 large fish cakes

6 medium Maris Piper potatoes, peeled and chopped
2 medium/large cod lion fillets (or you can use salmon, tuna or haddock)
50g butter
salt and freshly ground black pepper
2–3 tablespoons flat-leaf parsley, finely chopped
100g plain flour

Peel and chop the potatoes and steam until soft. (Or you could bake them in the oven and scoop out the middle.) Mash with the butter in a large bowl and season well.

Place the fish in a pan of boiling water over the heat for five minutes. Remove the fish from the water and flake the fish into the mash being careful to remove any bones and skin.

Add the parsley and combine the mixture well. Then, using your hands, form the mixture into 6 fish cakes.

Pat each fish cake with a little flour on either side and then brown them in a frying pan in a little oil.

Lightly grease a baking tray and place the fish cakes on the tray, then bake in the oven for 20 minutes, turning once halfway through.

Serve with a fresh salad. Kids may like them in a bun like a burger!

Sausage and Potato Omelette

You can't make an omelette without breaking eggs, so the saying goes. And every mother knows just how much fun breaking eggs can be for kids. So get them stuck in with this and you're on to a winner. Our take on the omelette is so simple – you don't even have to do the awkward turning bit – so you can be sure you won't end up with something more like scrambled eggs.

Serves 2–4

1 medium Maris Piper potato, peeled and cut into small chunks
2 tablespoons olive oil
½ large white onion, finely chopped
½ red pepper, seeds removed and finely sliced
6 pork sausages, cooked and sliced
4 large free-range eggs
100ml semi-skimmed milk
salt and freshly ground black pepper
100g mature Cheddar cheese, grated

Heat a frying pan over a medium heat with the olive oil and fry the potato chunks with the onion for about 5 minutes. Then add the red pepper and sliced sausage and continue to fry over a low to medium heat for another 10 minutes, until the potato is cooked. You may need to add a little more oil to prevent the vegetables sticking to the pan.

In a bowl, place the eggs and milk and whisk together well before seasoning with plenty of salt and pepper. Pour the eggs into the pan and tilt to make sure all the vegetables are covered with the egg mixture. Cook over a medium heat for a further 3–4 minutes, making sure that it doesn't burn underneath.

Remove the pan from the heat and sprinkle over the grated cheese. Place the frying pan under a hot grill for about 5 minutes until the top of the omelette has cooked and the cheese has turned golden brown.

To serve, lift the omelette out of the frying pan and serve with a crisp green salad.

Kiddies' Enchiladas

This dish is great for getting kids to eat food they think they don't like. The salsa, onions and peppers are so well hidden in the tortillas they won't even see the good stuff!

Serves 4

4 chicken breast fillets, cut into strips
1–2 tablespoons olive oil
1 tablespoon butter
1 large white onion, finely chopped
1 green pepper, seeds removed and
*   thinly sliced*
200g ready-made salsa sauce
200g mature Cheddar cheese, grated
2 tablespoons ground cumin
8 flour tortillas
200ml whipping cream
300ml chicken stock

Preheat the heat at 190°C /Gas 6.

Heat a frying pan over a medium heat with the olive oil and fry the chicken strips for about 20 minutes, or until cooked. Once cooked, cut and shred the chicken into pieces.

In a separate frying pan, melt the butter and add the chopped onion and sliced pepper and fry over a medium heat until soft. Once cooked, remove from the heat, add the chicken pieces, salsa, 50g of the cheese, ground cumin and mix together well.

Working with one tortilla at a time, lay the tortilla on a chopping board or plate and a heaped tablespoon of the mixture down one side and roll, folding the ends in and tucking underneath the enchilada. Place them in a lightly-greased baking dish. Repeat until you have used all the mixture.

In a bowl or jug, combine the whipping cream and chicken stock together. Sprinkle half the remaining cheese over the enchiladas and then pour over the chicken stock and cream mixture. Bake in the oven for about 20 minutes.

After 20 minutes of cooking time, sprinkle over the remaining cheese, return to the oven and bake for a further 10 minutes until the cheese is golden brown. Serve with chunky homemade wedges or a fresh green salad.

Home-MAde PiZZa

Children and pizzas are a match made in heaven. And you don't often find a child who isn't creative. With these things in mind, we suggest you get them involved in making pizza from start to finish. Give them their own piece of dough and let them get on with it, guiding them when necessary.

Makes 3 small individual pizzas

For the base
7g pack of yeast
300ml tepid water
500g bread flour
1 tablespoon olive oil

For the pizza sauce
1 large white onion, finely chopped
1 x 400g tin chopped tomatoes, drained
$1/_2$ teaspoon ground basil
1 clove garlic, crushed
2 tablespoons tomato purée
1 teaspoon of granulated sugar
salt and freshly ground black pepper, to taste
150g mature Cheddar cheese, grated (or you can try goat's cheese for an adult version, crumbled)

Preheat the oven at 180°C /Gas 5.

First, make the pizza base. Pour the yeast into a jug and add 300ml of tepid water, stir gently to combine, then leave for 30 minutes until frothy.

Once the yeast is frothy, pour the flour into a large mixing bowl and make a well in the centre. Pour 100ml of the yeast mixture into the hole and fold gently into the flour.

Continue adding the yeast mixture a little at a time until you have a smooth dough. You may find that you do not have to use all the yeast mixture. In the bowl, knead the dough with your hands for a few minutes to thoroughly bring it together.

Mould the dough into a ball and place in the bottom of a separate, lightly-oiled bowl. Cover with cling film and place the bowl in a warm environment for about 20 minutes to allow the dough to rise. (An airing cupboard is perfect!)

Once the dough has doubled in size, take it out of the bowl and cut into 3 even pieces. Lightly flour a clean work surface and roll each ball of dough out to form three pizza bases. Lightly flour a baking tray and place the pizza bases on the baking tray.

To make the pizza sauce, heat a frying pan over a medium heat with a little olive oil and sauté the onions for about 5 minutes. Add the rest of the sauce ingredients, turn the heat down to low and allow to simmer for a further 5–10 minutes, until the onions are completely soft. Remove from the heat and dollop spoonfuls of the sauce on top of each of the pizza bases and spread out evenly. Sprinkle 50g of cheese over each pizza.

It is entirely up to you what toppings you want to put on top of your pizza, but try and encourage your kiddies to add some fresh, healthy ingredients while having a little fun with it; sliced red peppers to make a smiley face, sweet corn for hair, pineapple for eyebrows and even a fried egg in the middle for a nose.

Once you have added your pizza toppings, place in the oven for 10–15 minutes until the cheese is golden brown and the toppings cooked through.

Mocktails for kids

Obviously we're not for a minute suggesting you ply your children with gin. We're talking about delicious virgin cocktails. Serve them with an umbrella, a straw and a swizzle stick and they'll think you're super cool.

Shirley Temple
Fill a highball glass with ice. Add a couple of dashes of grenadine and fill with ginger ale. Add a twist of lemon peel and a slice of orange to the glass.

Gentle Sea Breeze
Mix equal measures of cranberry and pineapple juice and pour into a glass filled with crushed ice. Decorate with a sprig of mint.

Coconut Colada
Mix two parts pineapple juice to one part coconut milk and place with lots of ice into a blender and whizz until mixed. Pour into a chilled glass. Garish with an orange slice and some cherries on a cocktail stick.

Mint choc chip
Pour one part peppermint cordial and four parts milk into a blender. Add a scoop of chocolate ice cream and some ice cubes and whizz until blended. Pour into a glass and grate over some milk chocolate.

RASpberry Muffins

Muffins are so easy to make and don't require the kind of precision mixing other cakes demand, and so are perfect for little ones to have a go at making. Some children reject raspberries because of their sourness, but these muffins are light and sweet and an excellent way to get kids to eat fruit.

Makes about 8 muffins

For the muffins
50g butter
70g caster sugar
2 medium free-range eggs
150g plain flour
2 tablespoons baking powder
2 tablespoons vanilla essence
150g raspberries

For the icing
80g icing sugar
1 teaspoon pink or red food colouring (optional)
1–2 tablespoons water
a small handful of raspberries, to decorate

8 muffin cases

Preheat the oven at 170°C/Gas 4.

Set out the muffin cases in a muffin tray.

Into a large mixing bowl, add the butter and sugar and whisk with an electric whisk until thick and creamy. Then add one egg at a time, whisking in between each one until thoroughly combined. Next, add the flour, baking powder and vanilla essence and whisky again until thoroughly mixed.

Add the raspberries to the mixture and stir to combine. Spoon the batter into the prepared muffin cases, being sure to divide the mixture evenly between each.

Bake in the oven for 18–20 minutes until well risen and golden on top. Remove from the oven and leave to cool completely.

Once the muffins are completely cool, make the icing. In a small bowl, mix the icing sugar with the water and food colouring (if using) to form a thick paste. Spoon a little of the icing on top of each muffin and let it drip down the sides. Finish by garnishing with a fresh raspberry on top.

Silly Banana Split Face

It's a strange fact, but children love their food to smile at them. Who hasn't laid out supper in a huge grin to encourage their child to eat that little bit more. Go one step further and let the children make their own smiley face with this fun pudding.

Makes 2 banana splits

2 bananas, peeled, cut in half and then half again for the hair and mouth
4 medium scoops ice cream, any flavour, for the eyes
4 strawberries, hulled and cut in half for the nose
200g milk chocolate buttons, for the pupils and the teeth
squirty cream, for the mouth

To assemble the banana split faces, arrange 3 of the quarters of banana at the top of each plate to create the hair. Place two scoops of ice cream under the hair for the eyes, adding a chocolate button on top of each ice cream scoop for the pupils.

Pile the strawberries in the middle of the plate to make a nose and use the remaining banana quarter for the mouth, adding some squirty cream along the length of the banana and then decorating with more chocolate buttons, for teeth.

How to Cook in High Heels

Children's Party Menu

OK, firstly don't knock yourself out. Children get far too excited to eat a lot at a party and, if you make too much, you'll be eating it for weeks. Remember, retro plays well with small children – it's all new to them!

Sticky sausages
Preheat the oven to 200°C/gas mark 6. Pop 20 cocktail sausages in a roasting tin lined with baking parchment. Brush them with three tablespoons of runny honey and cook for about 25 minutes until they're cooked through and a lovely dark brown.

Cheese and pineapple hedgehog
Cover half a grapefruit in foil. Open a tin of pineapple chunks and chop a block of cheese into cubes. Thread each cocktail stick with one pineapple chunk and one cheese cube and stick it into the foil-covered grapefruit. Repeat until your hedgehog takes shape. Use three black grapes as the eyes and a glacé cherry for the mouth.

Sandwiches
Marmite, peanut butter and jam sandwiches tend to go down best. Be creative, though, by using one slice of white and one of brown for each sandwich and use a cookie cutter to make them into shapes.

Fairy Cakes
Preheat the oven to 200°C/gas mark 6. For 12 cakes, you need 125g each of soft butter, caster sugar and self-raising flour. You also need two eggs and half a teaspoon of vanilla extract. Throw everything into a food processor and whizz until smooth. Bake for 15-20 minutes until they're golden, have risen and are cooked through. Allow to cool. For the icing: sift some icing sugar into a bowl and mix with a little hot water or fruit juice until it makes a thick icing. If it gets too runny add more icing sugar; too thick more water. Spread over your fairy cakes and top with a single crystallised rose, a Smartie or a jelly bean or buy a tube of writing icing and personalise each cake with a message.

Mini Muffins
Muffins always go down a treat at parties. Buy some mini muffin cases and turn them into bite-sized treats. See page 88 for the recipe.

The Cake
There really isn't space to offer a recipe here and, frankly, birthday cakes are a book in their own right. Our advice, born out of experience, is that the cake is where you should direct your attention. You needn't rush out and buy a hideously expensive cake, but you should spend a lot of time researching to find something with a theme your child will appreciate.

Drinks
Avoid, at all costs, anything fizzy or orange squash that contains tartrazine. In our experience, you'll end up with hyperactive children who either howl loudly or worse! Serve juice or, if you're catering for older children, a selection of the mocktails on page 88.

The FOOd of LoVE

You know someone loves you when they've gone to the effort of cooking you a delicious supper and eating at home can be far more romantic than a trip to a fancy restaurant. There's an intimacy that's kind of sexy in the act of cooking for someone.

First things first, you don't need to labour over some hugely extravagant seven-course extravaganza. In fact, if you do you'll end up hot and frazzled and won't enjoy the evening at all. He wants to gaze into your eyes over the table, not watch you dashing into the kitchen every five seconds.

Whether your relationship is brand new or you've been together forever, talking to each other over a candlelit table and plates of something delicious is sure to put you both in a romantic mood. After all, life is hectic and sometimes it's lovely to just take time out for each other.

Quiet, leisurely, uninterrupted moments are the glue that binds you together and making an effort by cooking will show him just how important he is to you.

Atmosphere is important, too. So light some candles, dig out some CDs of romantic music, step into your sexiest shoes and enjoy every second...

Warming up

Food and romance go hand in hand. Here are a few ideas to get you started...

Have a picnic. Spread a blanket under a tree, either in your garden or in the park, and wile away the afternoon. In the winter make it a carpet picnic indoors, preferably in front of an open fire.

Rather than complaining about him watching the football, make his favourite food and serve it on a tray. Just don't expect any thanks until the match is over! Besides, he might be more inclined to do the same for you when *Sex And The City* is on!

The seaside is made for romance, but there's something truly special about it at dusk during the last days of summer. Eat fish and chips out of the paper and drink mini bottles of champagne. Bliss!

Get up early, make bacon rolls and a flask of coffee and watch the sun rise together.

Camp out under the stars and cook your supper over an open fire. Fish with a few simple herbs and baked potatoes tastes delicious eaten outdoors.

Make him breakfast in bed – boiled eggs with asparagus soldiers is the perfect romantic dish.

Baked Figs
and Goat's Cheese Salad

The sweetness of the figs is the perfect foil for the tang of the goat's cheese and this dish couldn't be easier to assemble, leaving you lots of time to get ready...

Serves 2

2 large fresh figs, bases cut in a cross
  slit almost to the bottom
50g good quality soft goat's cheese
2 tablespoons pine nuts
2 large handfuls of rocket and
  watercress

For the dressing
1 tablespoon balsamic vinegar
3 tablespoons olive oil
1 teaspoon Dijon mustard
1 teaspoon brown sugar

Preheat the oven at 175°C /Gas 4.

First, place the figs on a small baking tray. Fill the split cavities with the goat's cheese and sprinkle over the pine nuts. Place in the oven for about 10–15 minutes, until the figs become a little gooey and the cheese has melted.

To make the dressing, mix the vinegar, oil and mustard together in a small bowl.

To serve, arrange the rocket and watercress leaves on two serving plates, place one fig in the middle of each and drizzle with the dressing. Serve while warm with a chunk of fresh crusty bread for mopping up the juices.

How to Cook in High Heels

Grilled Oysters with Tabasco

Synonymous with romance, oysters are a well-known aphrodisiac and when you serve this your intentions will be clear...

Serves 2

8 fresh oysters, opened and left in their shells
2 tablespoons flat-leaf parsley, finely chopped
2–3 garlic cloves, finely chopped
2 tablespoons olive oil
Tabasco sauce, to taste
1 lemon, cut into wedges, to serve

First you need to open the oysters (the trickiest part of this recipe we promise!) If you have an oyster opener, use this. If not, get a flat-edged knife and gently insert the tip into the corner of the shell near the hinge, taking care not to insert the knife too far. Gripping the shell firmly (you may also prefer to hold it with a tea towel in case the knife slips), gently slide the knife around the edge of the shell to loosen it. Using the tip of the knife as a lever, twist the blade slightly to open the shell. Discard the top half of the shell.

Place the oysters in their shells on a baking tray and sprinkle evenly with the chopped parsley and garlic. Drizzle each oyster with a little olive oil and a few dashes of Tabasco sauce. Place under the grill on a medium heat for about 10–15 minutes, until the garlic begins to brown.

Serve with lemon wedges – delicious!

GinGer & LiME SmOked SaLmOn with AVoCado

Smoked salmon is a bit of a luxury, so always feels rather spoiling, and ginger has just the right amount of kick to wake up your senses. This dish offers the perfect start to a romantic supper for two…

Serves 2

2¹/₂–5cm piece of fresh ginger, peeled and grated
juice of ¹/₂ lime
200–300g smoked salmon
2–3 tablespoons coriander, finely chopped
¹/₂ avocado, peeled and sliced
4 slices crusty brown bread, to serve

In a bowl, combine the grated ginger, lime juice and chopped parsley and mix well. Toss the smoked salmon pieces in the mixture until they are thoroughly coated. Arrange the salmon on a serving place with some sliced avocado and serve with crusty brown bread.

Creating a romantic atmosphere

OK, so you've decided to cook a romantic supper. You've planned the menu, chosen your dress and now all you need to do is get the atmosphere right...

Beg, steal or borrow a babysitting favour and get a friend to have the children overnight.

Candlelight creates the perfect atmosphere. It changes the everyday into something special. And we all look gorgeous bathed in soft light.

Music really sets the mood. Try some late-night smokey jazz.

Scatter rose petals over the table. Red looks amazing on a white tablecloth.

Turn off the TV – nothing kills passion quite as much as a re-run of Top Gear or the latest installment of America's Next Top Model.

And, while we're turning things off, do the same with your computer, mobile phone or Blackberry.

Nuts About you Chicken

Cooking a romantic dinner needn't cost the earth, as this dish shows. It tastes delicious and is perfect for a cosy night in (and is packed full of aphrodisiac ingredients such as chilli, garlic and cashew nuts too!).

Serves 4–6

1 large white onion, finely chopped
2 garlic cloves, finely chopped
1 large red chilli, deseeded and finely chopped
1–2 olive oil
8 medium chicken thighs, skinned, boned and cut into chunks
1 butternut squash, peeled, deseeded and chopped into large chunks
400ml chicken stock
salt
freshly ground black pepper
90g cashew nuts
2–3 tablespoons coriander, finely chopped
millet, basmati rice or creamy mash potato to serve

Heat a deep saucepan over a medium heat and lightly fry the onion, garlic and chilli in a little olive oil until soft.

Add the chicken to the onion mixture and fry for 1–2 minutes to seal the meat. Then add the butternut squash to the saucepan along with the chicken stock so that the stock just covers the contents of the pan. Bring to simmering point and cook for about 20 minutes, until the chicken is cooked through and the butternut squash has softened. Season well with salt and pepper.

Heat a non-stick frying pan over a medium heat and toss in the cashew nuts. Lightly toast the nuts for 1–2 minutes until brown, being sure to keep the pan moving to avoid the nuts burning.

To serve, sprinkle the chicken and butternut squash with the toasted cashew nuts. Serve alongside millet, basmati rice or creamy mashed potato.

Chilli and Ginger Fillet Beef with Wild Rice

This dish is so delicious that he's guaranteed to fall in love with you all over again.

Serves 2

1 carrot, peeled and sliced lengthways
400g beef fillet, cut into two pieces
4 tablespoons sesame oil
8 tablespoons dark soy sauce
3cm chunk of fresh ginger, peeled and grated
¹/₂ large red chilli, deseeded and finely chopped
120g mixed wild and basmati rice
1–2 tablespoons olive oil
3 spring onions, finely chopped
2 tablespoons pine nuts

First, marinate your beef fillets. Place the beef in a shallow dish or bowl and combine with the carrot, sesame oil, soya sauce, grated ginger and chilli, cover, and refrigerate for at least one hour. Don't leave for more than 2 hours however, or the beef will become too salty.

Meanwhile, bring a saucepan of water to the boil and cook the rice according to the instructions on the packet. Drain, and set aside.

Heat a frying pan over a medium heat and fry the spring onions and pine nuts in the olive oil for 3–4 minutes. Mix these in with the rice.

Next, remove the beef from the marinade. Heat a non-stick frying pan over a medium to high heat and fry the beef for about 5 minutes, being sure to seal it well on all sides (you can add a little oil to the pan if it looks like the beef is sticking too much). Before the beef cooks through, add the marinade to the pan and cook for a further few minutes, allowing the marinade to reduce slightly. Remove from the heat.

Take the beef out of the pan, slice thinly and arrange on a serving plate. Spoon the rice into clean martini or cocktail glasses and press down, then turn out onto the plate to form a pyramid shape next to the beef. Drizzle over the marinade and serve.

HaM, ChickEN and ASpaRagus Pie with CeleRiac MaSh

What could be more romantic than baking a pie for your man? Packed full of delicious ingredients – including that well-known aphrodisiac, asparagus – he's sure to love this...

Makes 2–3 individual pies

1 large white onion, finely chopped
1–2 tablespoons olive oil
1 tablespoon plain flour
1/2 glass white wine
2 x 150g gammon steaks
1 medium roast chicken (about 750g)
2 tablespoons double cream
a small handful of flat-leaf parsley,
   finely chopped
salt
freshly ground black pepper
6–8 asparagus tips
400g ready-rolled puff pastry
1 medium free-range egg, beaten

For the celeriac mash
1 celeriac, peeled and cut into chunks
1 tablespoon butter
2 tablespoons full-fat milk
salt and freshly ground black pepper

Preheat the oven at 170°C /Gas 5.

Heat a frying pan over a medium heat with the olive oil and fry the onion for about 5 minutes or until soft. Add the flour and stir to coat the onion, then pour in the wine along with a little water and mix well. Once the sauce has thickened a little, remove from the heat.

Meanwhile, heat another frying pan over a medium heat and fry the gammon steaks in a little oil for about 3– 4 minutes, until cooked. Remove and chop into small pieces. Remove the skin and discard the bones from the chicken and break into pieces.

Return the pan with the onions to the heat and add both the gammon and chicken pieces to the onions and allow to cook for a couple of minutes over a medium heat. Add the cream and a little parsley, then season well with salt and pepper. Be careful not to add too much salt as the gammon is already quite salty. Add the asparagus tips and mix together well. Cook for a further 2 minutes, then remove from the heat.

Spoon the pie filling into 2–3 individual pie dishes. Cut out circles of puff pastry and lay over the tops of the pie dishes. Next, cut a strip of pastry long enough to wrap around the edge of the pie dish and press down gently with your fingers to seal the pastry.

To really give your pies that loving touch, cut out a small heart shape or the words 'I Love U' in the pastry. Arrange on top of the pastry lids and then brush with the beaten egg. Place the pie dishes on a baking tray and bake in the oven for 20 minutes, or until the puff pastry has risen and is golden brown.

While the pies are cooking, steam the celeriac pieces until soft. Transfer to a bowl and add the butter, milk, salt and pepper then mash until smooth.

Serve your 'love pie' with a big dollop of mash sprinkled with the freshly chopped parsley.

BOOZy CHoCoLaTe MoUssE

This rich, velvety chocolate mousse is unbelievably delicious and is sure to keep true love on course. You can substitute Tia Maria for his favourite liqueur. So if he loves oranges opt for Grand Marnier; if he's a coconut lover, go for Malibu; and if he loves mint, go for Crème de Menthe...

Serves 6 (enough for leftovers – if you have children, leave out the alcohol and you'll have pudding for them the next day)

250g dark chocolate (minimum 70% cocoa solids)
4 free-range egg yolks
8 large free-range egg whites
200g caster sugar
150ml whipping cream
25–35ml (1 standard shot) of Tia Maria
6 strawberries or raspberries, to decorate

First, bring a saucepan of water to the boil. Break the chocolate into a heatproof bowl and place over the pan of boiling water. Heat gently, stirring, until the chocolate has completely melted, being careful to ensure the bowl doesn't touch the water. Take the chocolate off the heat. In a mixing bowl, beat the egg yolks. Pour in the melted chocolate and mix until well combined, allowing the mixture to thicken.

In a bowl, beat the egg whites with an electric whisk until light and frothy. Next, add the sugar and continue whisking until very stiff peaks are formed when you lift the whisk out of the egg whites. This will take about 8 minutes, so stick with it or your mousse will be too runny!

Into another large bowl add the whipping cream and beat with the electric whisk until very thick. This should take about 5–6 minutes.

Fold the egg whites into the chocolate mixture until well combined. Add the whipped cream and Tia Maria and fold together until you have a smooth, even mixture.

To serve, spoon into champagne glasses and place in the fridge to set for at least 3 hours. Once set, remove from the fridge and garnish with the strawberries or raspberries just before serving.

Keeping romance alive

Think back to the early days of your relationship when you could barely keep your hands off each other and an hour spent apart felt like an eternity? If that feels like a distant dream then a few simple steps and a little effort is all it takes to rekindle the fires of passion...

We know you've heard this before, but make a date and stick to it. Put it in the diary and refuse to let anything interfere with the plan.

Send him a romantic or saucy text. Just letting him know you're thinking of him, will ignite a spark.

Make a real effort with how you look when he's around. It's all too easy to dress up for work or nights out with friends and to let yourself go at home. If he only sees you looking gorgeous as you're heading out the door, then how's he going to remember how lovely you really are?

The biggest passion-killer is lack of courtesy. It's amazing how many of us have impeccable manners when talking to the postman or our work colleagues, but can be unspeakably rude to our partners.

Really listen. In the early days – when we're desperate to know every last detail about his life – we really pay attention. When the relationship's a bit older, we tend to lose interest in what he's saying. But, if it's important enough for him to tell you, then it really matters to him.

Sparkling Raspberry Jelly

If you thought jelly was only for the kids, then you were wrong. This frivolous dish will leave you in no doubt that it's great for grown-ups too. The blush-pink colour and sparkling wine make it an ideal end to a romantic supper...

Serves 4–6

135g raspberry jelly
375ml cava
150g raspberries
squirty cream, to decorate

Break the jelly into a heatproof bowl. Add about 100ml of cold water and microwave according to the packet instructions. Stir, checking to make sure all the jelly has melted. Pour the cava into the bowl with the jelly and mix together well.

Put some raspberries in the bottoms of 4–6 champagne flutes or cocktail glasses and pour in the jelly evenly. Place in the fridge to set for about 3– 4 hours.

When you're ready to serve the jellies, remove from the fridge and decorate with squirty cream and another fresh raspberry on top. Devour!

Passion Fruit and Lemon Posset

Fun, flirty and definitely passionate, this light-as-a-feather dish rounds off a romantic dinner perfectly...

Serves 4

500ml double cream
200g caster sugar
juice and grated zest of 3 lemons
3 passion fruits, halved with the
    insides scooped out

Combine all the ingredients except the passion fruit in a saucepan and heat gently over a low heat for about 5 minutes, stirring often, until the sugar has completely dissolved.

Remove from the heat and sieve the mixture into a jug. Add nearly all the passion fruit to the sieved mixture (reserving a little for garnish), then discard the lemon zest in the sieve.

Pour into champagne flutes or very small serving bowls and place in the fridge to set for at least 2 $^1/_2$ hours.

When you're ready to serve the possets, spoon over the passion fruit seeds and serve with shortbread biscuits.

How to Cook in High Heels

Baileys and Chocolate-Covered Strawberries

Chocolate is universally linked with love and mix it with strawberries and a dash of Baileys and you've got the dreamiest dessert...

Serves 2

150g milk chocolate
50ml Baileys liqueur
400g strawberries

First, bring a pan of water to the boil. Break the chocolate into a heatproof bowl and place over the saucepan, being careful to ensure the bowl doesn't touch the water. Stir occasionally until the chocolate has melted.

Once the chocolate has completely melted, add the Baileys. If at this stage you find the chocolate mixture is too thick add a dash of milk to thin it out slightly. Be careful not to add too much milk or the chocolate will take longer to set.

Lay a sheet of baking parchment on a baking tray and set aside. Dip the fresh strawberries into the chocolate mixture and place on the tray. Once all the strawberries have been dipped, put the tray in the fridge to allow the chocolate to set for at least one hour, but the longer the better.

FinD Your InneR GoddEss

You see wobbly thighs and a bottom the size of a small country. He sees a vision of sexiness. Everyone is insecure about something, but we know for certain that when you're with a man, he is not for a second thinking about your imperfections!

If you've lost your mojo, think back to a time when you felt really gorgeous. Try to recreate those feelings in your mind and you'll begin to feel attractive again. Failing that, channel a woman you think is really hot. Strut like Madonna or slink like Cheryl Cole. We promise it works!

Don't fall into the trap of thinking you need to be over-the-top to be sexy. Many men are actually terrified of predatory women, find the idea of PVC rather intimidating and run a mile from women who boast about their conquests.

Learn to flirt. It's a subtle art and can be used to great effect. Hold his gaze for a moment longer than is decent, play with your hair, lean in when he's talking to you and speak softly, so he has to do the same and put your hand lightly on his arm when you're making a point.

Men love the thrill of the chase. Make it too easy and he'll lose interest. Make it too hard and the same will happen. The trick is to be just that little bit elusive. Don't be tempted to pick up the phone – wait for him to call you. Don't instantly reply to a text or email. Let him imagine you're out doing something fantastically exciting.

EnteRtaiNing

Gathering people together is huge fun and there's always an air of excitement when there's a party looming. Get-togethers provide the perfect opportunity for a little matchmaking or to make sure you catch the eye of your secret crush. The best parties are those which, while well organized, are laid back and informal and the secret lies in the planning.

Gatherings come in all shapes and sizes – from the smallest of kitchen suppers through to the biggest, wildest of parties and everything in between. We've made sure that we've included as much as space would allow and have covered all seasons. So you'll find great barbecue ideas, perfect canapés, starters, main courses and puddings for dinner parties and some brilliant ideas for Christmas entertaining too.

Cooking for friends – whether it's six or 60 – shouldn't be daunting, but even the calmest of cooks can get a little frazzled. That's why we've created recipes that are easy to follow and give you lots of time to get ready.

From tiny gatherings through to Christmas extravaganzas, brilliant barbecues and more, you'll find it all here. Plus, we've also included lots of useful tips on dressing up, decorating a table and much more to ensure your party goes with a bang!

Come Dine

Staying in is the new going out. But planning a dinner party can be a double-edged sword and can strike fear into the heart of even the bravest of girls. While you may love the idea of gathering a group of friends round the table, it can be daunting if you're not the most experienced of cooks. But it needn't be so. We've created recipes that don't take an age to cook and won't break the bank. So pick up the phone, invite your mates round and get cooking...

Avocado and Bacon Boats

Quick and easy to make, these boats actually look as if you've spent a lot of time and energy on them, so lap up the praise as your guests tuck in...

Serves 4

2 ripe avocados, halved, flesh scooped out and roughly chopped, skins reserved to serve in
4 rashers of back bacon, chopped
2–3 tablespoons flat-leaf parsley, finely chopped
80g of iceberg lettuce, roughly chopped
juice of 1/2 lemon
4 slices crusty bread, to serve

Heat a frying pan over a medium heat and with olive oil and fry the bacon pieces for about 8–10 minutes until golden brown. Set aside.

In a small bowl, combine the bacon pieces with the chopped avocado and most of the parsley and mix together well.

When you're ready to serve, fill the avocado shells half way with lettuce, then spoon in the avocado and bacon mixture. Sprinkle the lemon juice over and serve with a slice of warm crusty bread.

Hot Stuffed Mozzarella Tomatoes

This quick and easy dish offers a delicious twist on the classic tomato and mozzarella salad. Perfect as a starter or side dish...

Serves 4

For the tomatoes
4 large beef tomatoes
200g mozzarella, chopped (You could use goats cheese instead if you prefer)
sea salt
freshly ground black pepper

For the pesto
a small bunch fresh basil (reserving a few whole leaves for a garnish)
3–4 tablespoons olive oil
150g pine nuts
2–3 tablespoons Parmesan cheese, grated

Preheat the oven to 200˚C/Gas 7

If you don't want to make your own, you can, of course, use jarred pesto or pesto bought in a deli, but it's pretty easy to make if you have a blender or food processor.

To make your pesto, combine all the ingredients in a blender or food processor and blitz for about 30 seconds, or until you have a rough paste.

Next, prepare your tomatoes by slicing off the tops and placing them to one side. Scoop out the seeds and pulp from within the tomatoes, being careful not to break the sides. Dollop a good heaped tablespoon of the pesto into the hollowed tomatoes and stuff almost to the top with the chopped cheese. Add another tablespoon of pesto on top and replace the tomato tops as 'lids'.

Sprinkle the tomatoes all over with salt and pepper and place on a baking tray lined with greaseproof paper. Bake in the oven for about 15 minutes or until the tomatoes have gone soft and the cheese is melted and oozing out.

Serve with a sprig of fresh basil and a fresh green salad.

How to Cook in High Heels

Mushroom, Leek and Lardon Linguine

You can't beat a good pasta dish and this one is always a huge hit with guests. You can serve this cold, just use penne instead of linguine, or drop the pasta altogether and serve as a side dish with chicken or fish...

Serves 4

200g bacon lardons (or you can use 200g streaky bacon cut into chunks)
1–2 tablespoons olive oil
3 leeks, finely sliced
200g closed up mushrooms, finely sliced
500g linguine
200–250ml crème fraîche
salt
freshly ground black pepper
2–3 tablespoons Parmesan cheese, grated (optional)

Heat a frying pan over a medium heat with the olive oil and fry the bacon lardons until they start to brown. Add the leeks and mushrooms and fry for a further 5 minutes, or until they begin to soften.

Bring a saucepan of water to the boil, add the linguine and cook according to the packet instructions until *al dente*. Once cooked, drain and transfer to a large mixing bowl.

Add the leek mixture to the linguine while still hot. Mix in the crème fraîche and season well, then serve immediately with a sprinkling of Parmesan cheese (if using).

Dinner parties in a hurry

If you're planning a weekday dinner for friends, try these tips to ensure you don't end up frazzled...

Be prepared
Shop well ahead, so you don't find yourself in the supermarket desperately searching for an elusive ingredient 20 minutes before your guests are due to arrive and, if at all possible, prepare at least some of the food in advance.

Keep it simple
Your friends have come to see you and if you spend all evening in the kitchen, emerging looking hot and frazzled, then no one is going to have a brilliant evening. If you're cooking something new have a practice run a week or so in advance.

Keep the kids happy
It's an indisputable fact that if children know you're busy they want twice as much attention as usual. Draft in a friend to keep the kids occupied until bedtime. Once the kids are tucked up, you can read them a bedtime story and be back in the kitchen in no time.

Timing's everything
Never invite people too far ahead – no one likes to commit months in advance. Equally, be clear on timing. Try saying 7.30pm for 8pm – that way you know for sure that everyone will be there and ready to eat by 8.30pm.

Spicy PraWN COckTaiL

We love the humble prawn cocktail – it's fun, retro and the perfect start to any dinner party. In the Nolan household it's a treat saved for Christmas Day, but frankly it's perfect whatever the season. We've added some spice to give our take on this dinner party classic a bit of kick...

Serves 4

For the sauce

4 tablespoons salad cream or mayonnaise
1 tablespoon tomato ketchup
juice of 3 limes
1 medium red chilli, finely chopped (remove the seeds if you want to make it milder)

1 Cos lettuce, finely shredded
a large handful of watercress, shredded
260g king prawns, cooked and shelled
1 ripe mango, peeled and roughly chopped
1 avocado, peeled, stoned and roughly chopped

First, make your sauce. In a small bowl combine the salad cream, ketchup and the juice of two limes and mix well. Add the finely chopped chilli and mix again. Set aside.

Divide the shredded lettuce and watercress evenly between four large wine glasses. Add a layer of prawns into each, being sure to reserve 4 for decoration, then a large spoon of the sauce. Scatter in the chopped avocado and mango, being sure to divide it evenly between the glasses.

Finish with another layer of the shredded lettuce and watercress and top with another spoon of the sauce before garnishing with the reserve prawns and a lime wedge for each glass. Enjoy!

MUsseLs in a WhiTe WiNe and CreaM SaUce

This reminds us of lazy days on holiday in the south of France and adds a certain glamour to any gathering. Make sure you get good-sized mussels as tiny ones are so unpromising...

Serves 4

1–1.2kg live mussels
4 shallots, finely chopped
1–2 tablespoons butter
3 cloves garlic, finely chopped
4–5 tablespoons flat-leaf parsley, finely chopped
250ml white wine
125ml double cream
salt
freshly ground black pepper
crusty bread, to serve

First, you need to prepare the mussels. Check them carefully and discard any that are open, broken, or that do not close up after tapping them lightly on the work surface. Then de-beard them by removing the small protruding 'thread' (it helps to use the blunt edge of a paring knife, though be sure to pull it out instead of cutting it off). Next, give the mussels a good scrub and allow to soak for at least 10 minutes in cold water to purge them of any grit that might lay inside. Drain and set aside.

Meanwhile, heat a large saucepan over a medium heat with the butter and fry the shallots and garlic until soft. Add the parsley and wine, then the mussels and simmer, covered, for about 5 minutes. Be sure not to lift the lid during this time as you will cause the steam to escape.

Check to see that the mussels have opened (you may need to replace the lid and cook for a further minute if they are still opening). Carefully spoon the mussels into a large serving bowl, being sure to discard any that haven't opened and cover with foil to keep them warm, leaving the sauce in the pan. Stir the cream into the sauce and season well. Pour the sauce over the mussels and serve immediately with crusty bread.

Garlic and Ginger Prawns with Pea Puree

This is our signature dish and defines our cooking philosophy. Good quality fresh ingredients make this combination of flavours incredible. A chic little dish that looks good, tastes divine and is made in moments...

Serves 4

For the pea purée
400g frozen peas
150ml low-fat crème fraîche
1–2 tablespoons fresh mint, chopped
salt
freshly ground black pepper

For the prawns
6 spring onions, chopped
2 garlic cloves, chopped
5cm chunk fresh ginger, peeled and grated
1–2 tablespoons butter
420g king prawns, cooked and shelled
fresh mint leaves, to garnish

To make the pea purée, steam the peas from frozen for 5–10 minutes, until they are cooked through. Place the peas in a blender and add the crème fraîche, chopped mint, salt and pepper and blitz until smooth.

Heat a frying pan over a medium heat and add the butter. When the butter starts foaming, add the spring onion, garlic and ginger and fry for about 5 minutes, or until the onions begin to soften. Add the prawns and cook for a further 2 minutes, turning off the heat before they start to shrink.

To serve, dollop the pea purée onto serving plates then top with the prawns and garnish with a spring of fresh mint.

LiTTle AlmONd and AppLe Tarts

These individual tarts are utterly delicious. The almond paste is the same as the filling for an almond croissant or Gallet de Roi, the dessert traditionally eaten in France at New Year. We've used apples as they give a crispy texture and slightly tart flavour, but you could experiment with other fruits, such as mango, peach or apricot...

Makes 4 tarts

375g ready-rolled puff pastry
100g ground almonds
75g golden caster sugar
2 medium free-range eggs, beaten
50g butter, softened
5–7 drops of almond extract
2 Granny Smith apples, sliced
4 tablespoons brown sugar, for sprinkling
1 medium free-range egg, beaten

Preheat the oven at 170°C /Gas 4.

Spray a large baking tray with a light oil spray or grease lightly with butter.

Cut the pastry into quarters to make four equal squares, then lay them on the baking tray.

In a bowl, mix together the ground almonds, sugar, half of the beaten eggs, butter and almond extract to make a smooth paste.

Using a palette knife, spread the paste equally over each square, leaving a 1cm border around the edge.

Lay the sliced apples on top of each tart in a decorative way, making sure they don't overlap too much as they won't cook evenly. Sprinkle all over with the brown sugar.

Fold the edge of the pastry squares inwards slightly to create a half-centimetre border all the way around, then brush all the visible pastry lightly with the remaining beaten egg.

Place the tarts in the oven and bake for about 15 minutes until the apples are soft and starting to turn golden brown.

Serve warm with a huge dollops of vanilla ice cream!

Choc Chip Cookie Cream and Sherry Pie

This is the perfect ending to a dinner party, a Christmas get-together or a special Sunday lunch. It can be prepared the day before and the longer you leave it, the better it tastes...

Serves 6

750g chocolate chip cookies
250ml sweet sherry
600ml double cream
150 whipping cream, whipped
1 Flake chocolate bar, crumbled

Pour the sherry into a small bowl and dip each biscuit in the sherry. Lay half the biscuits on the bottom of a medium to large sized baking dish. Pour over half the double cream. Repeat this process using up the remaining biscuits and double cream ending in a layer of biscuits until the baking dish is almost full.

Spread a thick layer of the whipped cream over the top of the pie and sprinkle the broken flake on top for decoration. Chill in the fridge for at least a couple of hours before serving, but it's even better if left overnight!

Baked Bananas with Cinnamon and Orange

Serves 4

4 bananas, peeled and sliced
*   lengthways*
50g brown sugar
1 tablespoon of water
1 teaspoon ground cinnamon
juice of 1 orange
vanilla ice cream or crème fraîche, to
*   serve*

Preheat the oven to 180°C /Gas 5.

Lay the bananas in an ovenproof dish.

In a small bowl, mix together the brown sugar and water until smooth, but not runny (you may not need to add all the water).

Sprinkle the bananas with the ground cinnamon and then pour over the sugar mixture and orange juice, making sure each banana is covered evenly. Cover the baking dish with foil and bake in the oven for about 20 minutes, or until the bananas are soft and browning.

Serve the bananas hot with a few good scoops of the vanilla ice cream or crème fraîche.

BArbeCue

Summer is a brilliant season for entertaining. Fresh food is abundant and flavours and colours are vibrant. Light, healthy food is usually on the menu, which is a good thing when faced with the imminent prospect of a bikini. Barbecues are huge fun and a great way to entertain friends. All sorts of foods work well, not just the traditional sausages and burgers and now we're just as likely to barbecue fish, chicken and vegetables. Summer is, of course, salad season and there are so many delicious flavours that you can mix together to get even the most committed carnivore excited. These are the foods we love to serve on lazy summer days. So grab your friends, open a bottle of fizz and fire up the barbecue.

BakEd SeA BaSS
with FenneL

Stuffed fish is simple to prepare and is the perfect barbecue food. For us, this is the taste of summer...

Serves 4

4 whole sea bass, scaled and gutted (you could also use sea bream or Rainbow trout)
salt
2 tablespoons garlic paste or chopped fresh garlic
a small bunch fresh dill
1/2 fennel bulb, finely sliced
2 large tomatoes, sliced
a large handful of spinach
freshly ground black pepper

Rinse the fish and pat them dry with kitchen paper inside and out, then rub the salt into the skin of the fish.

Place each fish separately onto a large sheet of tin foil and spread $1/2$ tablespoon of garlic paste inside each. Stuff the dill, sliced tomatoes, fennel and spinach leaves between inside the cavities of the fish, being sure to divide the ingredients evenly between the four fish. Season well with freshly ground black pepper.

Bring the sides of the foil up around the fish – you may need another layer of tin foil – and wrap tightly. Place on top of the barbecue (or in the oven on 180°C /Gas 5) for 15–20 minutes until the fish is cooked through and the vegetables are soft.

How to Cook in High Heels

TaNdooRi CHicKen PiTTas
with a Yoghurt and Mint Dressing

These heavenly pockets are perfect eaten outdoors under a blazing sun. The cooling yoghurt is the perfect foil for the spicy chicken. If you're feeling virtuous, use wholemeal pitta bread...

Makes 24 pitta halves

6 chicken breasts, skinned and cut
  into chunks
juice of 1 lemon
3 tablespoons of tandoori or Tikka
  Masala curry paste
1 teaspoon garlic paste or chopped
  fresh garlic
1 teaspoon ginger paste or chipped
  fresh ginger
a small bunch of fresh mint, freshly
  chopped
5 tablespoons plain low-fat bio
  yoghurt
salt
freshly ground black pepper
$1/_2$ cucumber, peeled and grated
12 large pitta breads
150g mixed lettuce leaves

In a bowl, combine the chicken pieces and lemon juice and mix well. Add the curry paste, garlic, ginger, half the chopped mint, 2 tablespoons of the yoghurt and season well. Leave for at least 3–4 hours, but overnight is even better.

In another bowl, add the remaining yoghurt and mint and the grated cucumber, season well, and mix together thoroughly.

Divide the marinated chicken between 8–10 medium-sized squares of foil, wrapping the foil tightly around the chicken. Place on top of the barbecue for about 15 minutes, or until the meat is cooked.

Open up the pitta breads like pockets, then fill the bottoms with the mixed leaves and a few cubes of the chicken and top with a good dollop of the yoghurt dressing. Serve.

ScaLLop, ChoRizO and PePPer KebAbs

Kebabs are great – when the weather's hot it's nice to have something fairly light. Scallops and chorizo are made for each other and the red peppers add the perfect crunch...

Makes about 8 kebabs

24 scallops, shelled and cleaned
juice of 1 lemon
200g chorizo sausage, cut into about 24 thick slices
2 whole red peppers, seeds removed and cut into large chunks

8 wooden skewers that have been soaked in water for 2–3 hours, or even better, overnight

Preheat the oven to 180°C /Gas 5.

Place the scallops in a bowl and mix in the lemon juice. Leave aside to marinate, covered, for as long as possible, but at least one hour.

Place the chorizo sausage and peppers on a baking tray and bake in the oven for 5 minutes, to allow to cook through a little. Remove from the oven.

On to the skewers thread a chunk of pepper, slice of chorizo and a scallop and repeat this process until all the ingredients have been used. Lightly oil the kebabs all over.

Place on the barbecue and grill over the grill section, or if you don't have a grill section, place a layer of foil over the hot plate and cook directly on there.

How to Cook in High Heels

Beetroot, Carrot and Seed Salad

With grated carrots, raw beetroot and super seeds, this salad really is goodness on a plate. We prefer to use organic vegetables as they really do taste better and often cost no more than the non-organic variety...

Serves 6–8

6 large (preferably organic) carrots, peeled and grated
1–2 large (preferably organic) beetroots, grated
100g mixed seeds such sesame seeds, sunflower seeds and pumpkin seeds
juice of 2 lemons
6 tablespoons olive oil
1 tablespoon Dijon mustard
3 tablespoons balsamic vinegar
salt
freshly ground black pepper

In a large serving bowl, place the grated carrot and beetroot, then add the mixed seeds and the lemon juice and combine well.

In a separate bowl, mix together the olive oil, mustard and vinegar, then pour over the salad and season well with salt and pepper.

Allow to stand for at least an hour in the fridge to allow the flavours to infuse, but leave for longer if possible.

Parma Ham and Garlic Potato Salad

Potato salad is a summer staple, perfect for picnics as a side dish for barbecues or in lunchboxes. The garlic and ham give the dish a decidedly Mediterranean flavour...

Serves 6–8

1.3kg baby new potatoes, but into quarters
1 tablespoon cider vinegar
2 tablespoons wholegrain mustard
6 tablespoons low-fat mayonnaise
3 garlic cloves, finely chopped
3 shallots, finely chopped
4–5 tablespoons flat-leaf parsley, finely chopped
6 slices Parma ham or prosciutto, roughly chopped

Steam the potato quarters in a little water for 10–15 minutes, or until they are soft in the middle.

Meanwhile, in the bottom of a large serving bowl, mix together the vinegar, mustard and mayonnaise, then add the steamed potato and all the remaining ingredients and mix together well, ensuring that the potatoes are well covered with the dressing. Serve.

Sausage, Avocado and Sweet Chilli Wraps

Well, it wouldn't be a barbecue without a sausage or two. We've added a chic little twist to ensure everyone's happy...

Makes 16 tortilla halves

16 good-quality pork sausages, barbecued
8 flour tortillas
2 ripe avocados, peeled, stoned and sliced
150g rocket
sweet chilli dipping sauce, to serve

Grill the sausages on the barbecue until cooked through. Then lay two sausages in the middle of a tortilla wrap. Arrange a few slices of avocado alongside them, then add some rocket and a good splash of sweet chilli dipping sauce. Fold or roll the wrap tightly, cut in half and serve.

CiaBAtta BurGeRS with MoZZareLLa and sUN-bLusHed ToMAtoeS

Keep traditionalists happy by keeping burgers on the barbecue menu...

Makes 8 ciabatta burgers

For the burgers
500g lean minced beef
1 large white onion, finely chopped
1 medium free-range egg, beaten
1–2 tablespoons flat-leaf parsley,
    finely chopped
2 cloves garlic, crushed
1 tablespoon wholegrain mustard
salt
freshly ground black pepper

a little olive oil
4 large ciabattas
200g mozzarella, thinly sliced
16 sun-blush tomatoes, drained
150g spinach and watercress leaves
tomato ketchup, to serve
hot English or Dijon mustard, to
    serve

Place all the burger ingredients in a large mixing bowl and combine well with your hands. Form the mixture into approximately 8 balls (you will find this easier to do if your hands are slightly wet) and flatten slightly to make burgers. Refrigerate until you are ready to barbecue.

Lightly oil the burgers before placing them on the hot plate of the barbecue. Be sure to handle them gently when cooking as freshly-made burgers are more likely to fall apart than shop-bought burgers.

Cook the burgers on the grill section of the barbecue until thoroughly cooked. Chop roughly into pieces.

Slice the ciabattas in half, place in some of the chopped burger and top with some of the sliced mozzarella, a couple of sun blushed tomatoes, some spinach, watercress and either ketchup or mustard (or both). Place the ciabattas in a sandwich toasted and toast until the cheese has melted and the bread is warm. If you don't have a sandwich toaster, you can pop them under a hot grill for 5 minutes before serving.

MOrOCCan QuiNoa SaLad

This delicious salad is perfect served with barbecued meat and fish and is also great for picnics or a summer lunchbox...

Serves 6–8

300g quinoa
1 large white onion, finely chopped
1–2 tablespoons olive oil
100g raisins
100g apricots
200g hard goat's cheese, roughly
  chopped
100g walnuts, roughly chopped
the seeds from one fresh pomegranate
2–3 fresh mint, finely chopped
salt and freshly ground black pepper
2 tablespoons parsley, chopped

Cook the quinoa according to the instructions on the packet.

Heat a frying pan over a medium heat with the olive oil and fry the onion until just soft, then add the raisins and apricots and cook for a further 2–3 minutes, until they begin to soften as well.

Into a large serving bowl, add the chopped goat's cheese and walnuts, then add the fresh mint, quinoa onion mixture. Season well with salt and pepper, drizzle over a little good-quality olive oil and finish with a sprinkle of parsley.

CANaPEs

Over the next few pages are some of our favourite food ideas for drinks parties. These miniature snacks are perfect little hits of savoury and sweet to cater for a crowd. Just be sure to make enough because we guarantee they won't hang around for long!

Cheat's Beef Wellington

Beef Wellington is such a treat, but can be expensive if you're feeding a crowd. This miniature twist on the classic dish ensures a little goes a long way...

Makes 16

375g ready-rolled puff pastry
170g Brussels pâté
2–3 tablespoons horseradish sauce
1 medium free-range egg, beaten

Preheat the oven to 170°C /Gas 4.

Cut the pastry sheet into 16 even squares and do the same with the pâté. Place a square of pâté onto each square of pastry and press down slightly with the back of a spoon. Top each square of pâté with a small dollop of the horseradish sauce.

Brush the edges of the pastry with a little beaten egg, then fold each pastry square in half and press the edges together to seal the pastry.

Place the mini Wellingtons on a lightly-greased baking tray and brush the tops with a little more beaten egg.

Bake in the oven for 10–15 minutes, or until the pastry is golden brown.

Green-Lipped Mussels with Garlic and Cheese

Simple and delicious – just as party food should be.

700g Green Lip mussels (already opened)
2–3 tablespoons garlic paste or chopped fresh garlic
2–3 tablespoons Parmesan cheese, grated
2 tablespoons flat-leaf fresh parsley, finely chopped

First, you need to prepare the mussels. Check them carefully and discard any that are open, broken, or that do not close up after tapping them lightly on the work surface. Then de-beard them by removing the small protruding 'thread' (it helps to use the blunt edge of a paring knife, though be sure to pull it out instead of cutting it off). Next, give the mussels a good scrub and allow to soak for at least 10 minutes in cold water to purge them of any grit that might lay inside. Drain.

Place the halved mussels on a baking tray that has been covered in foil. Add a small dollop of the garlic paste on top of each mussel and a small sprinkle of Parmesan and chopped parsley.

Grill the mussels under a medium to high heat for 10–15 minutes, or until the cheese is bubbling slightly. Serve hot as delicious canapés.

How to Cook in High Heels

Bangers and Mash in a Shot

We love bangers and mash and serving a bite-sized version in a shot glass offers a cute twist on a great British classic...

Makes 24 shots

6 large Maris Piper potatoes, peeled and cut into chunks
1¹/₂ heaped tablespoons butter
2 tablespoons full fat milk
150g mature cheddar cheese, finely grated (you can vary this by using Blue Cheese if you prefer a slightly stronger flavour)
salt
freshly ground black pepper
24 good-quality cocktail sausages or mini chipolatas

Bring a saucepan of salted water to the boil and boil the potatoes for 10–15 minutes, or until the potatoes are soft when pierced with a knife. Drain and return the potatoes to the saucepan. Add the butter, milk and cheese and mash until smooth. Season well with salt and pepper. Set aside to keep warm.

Meanwhile, grill or fry the cocktail sausages or chipolatas for about 15 minutes, or until cooked.

Serve a small dollop of the creamy mash in a shot glass, complete with a chipolata (like an ice cream with a flake).

Perfect party dresses

Who hasn't trawled the shops – credit card in hand – only to find there are no suitable party dresses? Try these tips and you're sure to look super stylish...

Make the most of your assets
Stand in front of a mirror in a well-lit room and take stock of your body. Firstly, list your good points. Then think about the bits you're less keen on. Work with what you have – be it great legs, perfect cleavage, brilliant bottom – and maximise the positive and minimise the negative.

A good foundation
Lots of effort has gone into designing brilliant foundation garments, such as knickers and slips that will streamline your figure, smooth out any bumpy bits and give you a sleek silhouette. And, of course, there are bras that will upsize or downsize your bust. Use these brilliant inventions and you won't be sorry.

Accessorise
Costume jewellery is chic and funky and is a really cost-effective way of changing a look. A cocktail ring adds a touch of glamour, stacked bangles look great with a simple dress and a long necklace is brilliant for those of us who have a cleavage worth showing off.

True colours
Yes, yes, we know the little black dress is a classic for a reason. But it's easy to fall into the trap of only ever wearing black. It can be scary at first, so take things gently. Add a bright scarf, a wrap or a cardigan to your outfit and you'll be surprised how many people tell you how great you look.

The height of fashion
If you're tall then floor-length dresses can be rather flattering and look really elegant. But if you're petite, then you'll drown in all that fabric, so knee-length or higher is definitely best for you – and you'll be able to get away with a pair of killer heels without having to worry that you'll tower over the boys!

Make friends with a dressmaker
Let's face it, very few of us are a standard size and that's where a good dressmaker can really help. If you love a dress but it's a bit too long or too loose around the waist then your new best friend will be able to help. Also, she'll be able to help you with wardrobe updates, such as adding sleeves and customising pieces that are starting to look a little dated.

Sticky Toffee and Banana Filo Parcels

Make lots of these as your guests will be begging for more. Words cannot describe how utterly delicious these small parcels taste...

Makes 8–10 parcels

500g filo pastry
3–4 ripe bananas, peeled and sliced
250ml ready-made toffee sauce
1 medium free-range egg, beaten

Preheat the oven at 170°C/Gas 4.

Cut the filo pastry into squares by cutting through all the sheets at once, into quarters.

Top the centre of each square with some of the sliced banana and a small dollop of the toffee sauce. Brush the very edges of the pastry squares with a little beaten egg, then bring the sides up and squeeze tightly to stick the pastry together, forming parcels.

Place the parcels on a lightly-greased baking tray, brush with a little more beaten egg and bake in the oven for 10–15 minutes, or until the pastry is golden brown.

Serve whilst hot as a canapé, or with ice cream to make a delicious dessert.

Mini Trifles

These tiny individual trifles are sure to bring a smile to your guests' faces. Fun, appealing and pretty to look at, they're bound to be a huge hit...

Makes 16 cups

270g strawberry jelly
100g sponge fingers, broken into pieces
400g peach halves, cut into pieces
1kg carton of ready-made custard
1 can squirty cream
100g dark chocolate, grated

You will need about 16 medium wine glasses or you can buy throw-away plastic wine glasses or use any small transparent serving dishes.

First, prepare the jelly according to the packet instructions. Set aside.

Layer a few of the sponge finger pieces in the bottom of each glass and then sprinkle over some of the chopped peaches. Pour the jelly into the glasses to come about half way up, then place in the fridge to set. This will take 3–4 hours, so it's best to do them the day before.

Once the jelly has set, top with a layer of the custard, leaving just enough room for a layer of squirty cream at the top. Just before serving, add the cream and top with a little grated chocolate.

Cocktails

Cocktails are heaven in a glass and there are few things quite as fun as giggling with friends over a boozy confection...

Summer Chic

An afternoon in the garden with the girls, or a high-heeled trip to the park on a sunny day. Wherever you may be heading for those girly drinks this cocktail will leave you feeling fruity and glowing. Just be careful on those heels after!

Per Glass

25ml Bacardi
25ml Malibu
50ml orange juice
50ml pineapple juice
1 shot of blue caraco

Shake in a cocktail shaker, serve over crushed ice.

Cherry Bakewell

Aptly named as when mixed correctly this is exactly what it tastes like. Sinful? Yes. Worth it? Absolutely...

Per Glass

25ml Amaretto
25ml baileys
1 tablespoon of red grenadine

Pour the ingredients in this order into a short glass, using a spoon to guide a thin layer of grenadine onto the top. Do not stir.

Simply drink and enjoy.

Blue Dreams

With its blue colouring it's a constant reminder of being by the sea, whether it be in the winter months or the start of the summer. This drink can take you back to happy times you had in the sun or get you ready for good things to come!

Per Glass

25ml vodka
25ml blue caraco
a generous squirt of lime
100ml lemonade

Shake well in a cocktail shaker and serve in a tall glass over crushed ice. Refreshing!

CHrisTmas

The halls are decked, the presents wrapped, the turkey's ordered and it is most definitely the season to be jolly. So what's left to do, but throw a party?

MuSHrooMs with CHestnuT, BaCon and APPle STuffing

What would Christmas be without a little stuffing? These mushrooms are sure to get your guests in a festive mood...

To make 8 mushrooms

1 medium white onion, finely chopped
1–2 tablespoons olive oil
6 rashers smoked bacon, finely chopped
1 large cooking apple, finely chopped
4 slices of slightly stale bread
a small handful of fresh sage leaves, finely chopped
400g vacuum-packed chestnuts, roughly chopped
salt
freshly ground black pepper
1 tablespoon butter
8 Portobello mushrooms

Preheat the oven to 200°C /Gas 7.

Heat a frying pan over a medium heat with the olive oil and lightly fry the onion until soft, then add the bacon and fry until almost cooked through. Add the chopped apple and cook until soft, but not mushy.

Into a bowl, crumble the stale bread to make breadcrumbs and combine with the chopped sage and chestnuts, then season well. Tip the onion mixture into the bowl and add the butter. Mix thoroughly – the mixture should be slightly sticky.

Place the mushrooms upside down on a baking tray lined with greaseproof paper. Spoon the mixture onto the underside of the mushrooms, being sure to divide it evenly. Press the mixture down a little to hold it in place.

Bake in the oven for about 15 minutes, or until the mixture begins to brown on top and the mushrooms are softened. Serve immediately. This dish also works well as a starter with a fresh green salad or as a side dish.

The season to be jolly...

Sadly, Christmas has become horribly commercialised, but for us it's the traditions that surround the festive season and the small touches that make it all the more special...

Stir-up Sunday
We begin to feel a little festive on stir-up Sunday, the last Sunday before advent. Traditionally it's the day you make your Christmas pudding. It's great to get the kids into the kitchen helping you stir the pudding.

Deck the halls
Once the decorations are up, you really know it's Christmas. But rather than buying them, why not let the children get involved with making them. The school holidays can drag a bit in the run up to the big day, so arming the kids with some Christmas wrapping paper and a glue stick is a great way to keep them occupied, with the added benefit that you'll have miles of paper chains that can be used all over the house. They look particularly good over banisters and around windows.

All wrapped up
Rather than buying printed wrapping paper, why not make your own.
Buy lots of brown paper and customise it with ribbons or glitter or hand-print it with something personal to the recipient.

Mistletoe
Perhaps the best Christmas tradition of all. Place mistletoe all over the house to ensure romance blossoms throughout the festive season. Plus, put a sprig in your bag in case you see a gorgeous man on the bus or in the queue for the bank. Well, it is Christmas…

Smoked Salmon and Cucumber Tortillas

These little bites are ridiculously easy to make, taste delicious and won't have you piling on the pounds...

To make a large plate of tortilla slices

3–4 soft flour tortillas
200g low-fat cream cheese
300g smoked salmon, cut into strips
1/2 cucumber, finely sliced lengthways
1–2 tablespoons fresh chives, finely chopped

Spread each tortilla with some cream cheese right to the edges. Lay over pieces of the smoked salmon and cucumber and roll the tortillas up tightly. Seal the end with a little cream cheese if necessary.

Slice the tortillas up into bite-sized pieces and arrange on a large serving platter before sprinkling over the fresh chives.

Duck and Mandarin Christmas Curry Cups

Curry is universally popular and these curry cups are a real Christmas cracker! Cups are brilliant to serve party food such as curry and chilli in as it makes them really easy to eat...

To make 8 cups

1–2 tablespoons olive oil
1 large white onion, finely chopped
2 tablespoons mild curry paste
4 duck breasts, sliced
400g mandarin segments
8 heaped tablespoons plain low-fat yoghurt

Heat a frying pan over a medium heat with the olive oil and fry the onions until soft. Add the curry paste and cook for a few minutes. Then add the slices of duck and fry for a further 2 minutes to seal the meat.

Meanwhile, drain the mandarin segments from their syrup and add them to the pan, reserving a few to garnish. Mix thoroughly, reduce the heat and simmer for a further 15–20 minutes, or until the meat is tender.

Serve the curry in small tea cups and top with a teaspoon of yoghurt and a mandarin segment.

Santa's Satay Skewers

Our seasonal take on satay means we're using turkey instead of chicken. Well it is Christmas...

Makes 9–10 skewers

3–4 turkey breasts, skinned and sliced into strips
2 heaped tablespoons crunchy peanut butter
150ml sweet chilli sauce

10 wooden skewers, soaked for 3–4 hours or, even better, overnight.

Preheat the oven to 180°C /Gas 5.

Thread the strips of turkey breast evenly onto the skewers.

In a small bowl, mix together the peanut butter and sweet chilli sauce. Spoon over the turkey skewers, being sure to coat them thoroughly.

Bake in the oven for about 15 minutes until the turkey is thoroughly cooked, basting the turkey with the sauce half way through.

Serve hot.

How to Cook in High Heels

PoTatO SkiNs
with CrANBerry and GOaT's CHeese

Nothing says Christmas quite as loudly as cranberries and stuffed potato skins are great for parties – they're easy to make, taste delicious and are easy on the budget…

Makes 12 potato halves

6 medium/large baking potatoes
2–3 tablespoons olive oil
salt
2 tablespoons butter
2 heaped tablespoons low-fat crème fraîche
150g strong goat's cheese, chopped into small chunks
50g pine nuts
50g cranberries (dried or fresh)
2–3 tablespoons fresh mint, finely chopped
freshly ground black pepper

Preheat the oven to 200°C /Gas 7.

Wash and dry the potatoes and prick them all over with a fork. Rub them in the olive oil and sprinkle them with salt. Place them on a baking tray and bake in the oven for about an hour, or until the potatoes are soft in the middle when pierced with a knife.

Remove the potatoes from the oven, slice them in half and leave to cool for 10 minutes. Scrape out the potato flesh and place in a mixing bowl and place the potato skins on a baking tray. Add the butter and crème fraîche to the potato and mash until smooth. Add all the other ingredients and mix together well.

Spoon the potato mixture back into the potato skins, place back in the oven and cook for about 10–15 minutes, or until brown on top.

Serve while warm as canapés, a light lunch with a fresh green salad, or as part of a Christmas buffet.

How to Cook in High Heels

PaRTY PLannING

We love parties – our own or anyone else's – and over the years we've learned a few lessons that ensure a night to remember...

Mix it up
Invite a mixture of singles and couples, old friends and new and always say yes if someone asks to bring an extra guest. All of the above ensure for a fun night and interesting conversation.

Theme for dream
If you're planning a big party or it's for a special occasion, then consider having a theme. It can be as simple as black and white or as complicated as you like. Among our favourite themes are Heroes and Villains, Hollywood – complete with red carpet – Studio 54, Festival and X-Factor.

Any excuse for some fun
Sometimes it can be a bit daunting to throw yourself a birthday party, but it's always fun to do it for someone else. So you and your friends could take turns hosting each other's celebrations. Alternatively, why not throw a party to celebrate the first day of summer, getting a promotion or even just the fact it's the weekend. Many countries celebrate name days, so if you've been given the name of a saint why not check out the date you should be celebrating. Sadly, as yet, there's no St Sasha or St Korin, so we can't use this as an excuse for a party.

Pot luck (potlatch) suppers
These are particularly popular in America and brilliant if you're frantically busy, are on a tight budget or, like many of us, both. Each guest brings a dish to contribute to the table and you all tuck in. Simple, effective and often huge fun, this kind of get-together is great for close friends.

Safari suppers
If you're lucky enough to live in a village or a community with great neighbours, why not throw a safari supper. The concept is simple: you simply go to a different house for each course. You all sit down to eat your starter at the first neighbour's house and move on to the next for the main course and then another for pudding. You can make it last even longer by adding pre-dinner drinks and coffee to the itinerary.

Summer fun
We're not exactly blessed with the best of climates here, so it makes sense to enjoy every second of sunshine on offer. Barbecues are great fun – and rather restful as there's usually a man on hand desperate to drive the barbecue – and can be as simple or extravagant as you like. But why not make a weekend of it and have a mini festival in your garden? Get your friends to bring a tent, a guitar, harmonica or triangle and have two days of great food, music and fun.

OUR LittLE bLACk bOOk

Here we aim to put you in touch with some of the people and places that have looked after us so well over the years. It's a thank you list as much as it is a list of must-try recommendations.

You'll find everything from how to get the perfect smile, to the perfect body through to the chicest hotels and the most memorable restaurants. Just tell them we sent you!

Phone 020 7193 3448
www.harleystreetsmileclinic.co.uk
info@harleystreetsmileclinic.co.uk

Teeth whitening – a beautiful smile can transform your whole face!

Victoria Kendrick
Phone 07985 297344
www.victoriakendrickmakeup.co.uk
victoriakmakeup@yahoo.co.uk

For beautiful make up why not try our very own make-up artist? Vicky bases herself in London and the Midlands. Victoria also supplies us with all our jewellery. For a stockist sheet e-mail frillylillygroup@googlemail.com.

Manic Hair
90 Dartford Road
Dartford DA1 3ER

Phone 01322 284 151

For hair extensions that look amazing all year round and service with a smile be sure to this place gets my vote every time.

Rafayel's River Wellbeing Spa
34 Lombard Road, London SW11 3RF

Phone 0207 801 3610
www.hotelrafayel.com
reservations@hotelrafayel.com

We love this place. They're in Battersea and are perfect for Mum-and-Daughter days. Try their hot stone massage for the ultimate relaxation treat.

Phone 020 7314 4000
www.floridita.co.uk

Based in the heart of Soho, this place is perfect for a girls' night out. Wonderful atmosphere, great entertainment, Latino dancing and superb cocktails and food all night long! You can also find Floridita in Madrid, Dublin and Havana (so you can salsa your way around the world).

Studio Valbonne
62 Kingly Street
London W1B 5QN

Phone 0207 434 0888
www.studiovalbonne.co.uk
info@studiovalbonne.co.uk

One of the best London nightclubs around, situated in the West End and the perfect place to throw that oh-so-impressive kind of party.

Lucy's on a Plate
Church Street, Ambleside,
Cumbria LA22 0BU

Phone 015394 31191
www.lucysofambleside.co.uk

For truly wholesome, homely and delicious food this is a superb little café by day and restaurant by night.

The Botanist at Sloane Square
Phone 020 7730 0077
www.thebotanistonsloanesquare.com

For a fabulous girl's-only lunch, we recommend this place.

Phone 020 7383 3346
www.archipelago-restaurant.co.uk
info@archipelago-restaurant.co.uk

For a unique and exotic dining experience, we think this place is a must-visit. A real feast for the eyes and the stomach with a wonderful and unusual array of global cuisine on offer.

The Greenhouse
27a Hays Mews, Mayfair,
London W1J 5NY

Phone 0207 499 3331
www.greenhouserestaurant.co.uk
reservations@greenhouserestaurant.co.uk

For a romantic night with your partner, the Greenhouse is perfect to add a touch of romance.

The Crazy Bear Group

www.crazybeargroup.co.uk

For the most amazing Thai dining, delicious cocktails and beautiful hotel rooms – a luxurious experience. Can be found in Beaconsfield, Oxfordshire and London.

Triyoga
Phone 020 7483 3344
www.triyoga.co.uk

(Primrose Hill)
6 Erskine Road, London NW3 3AJ

(Soho)
2nd Floor, Kingly Court, London
W1B 5PW

(Covent Garden)
Wallacespace, 2 Dryden Street
London WC2E 9NA

For perfect wellbeing, health and
beautifully toned, stretched limbs,
Triyoga offer an extensive array of
yoga and pilates classes for all ages
and abilities including pregnant
women and children.

Fitness Boot Camp

Phone 0800 047 0488 or
+34 634053604
www.fitness-boot-camp.com
info@fitness-boot-camp.com

Looking to get back in shape? we
highly recommend the fitness boot
camp in Spain, beautiful scenery and
an amazing workout.

The Purple Dragon
Alexandra Avenue, Battersea
London SW11 4FN

Phone 020 7801 8688
www.purpledragonplay.com

Somewhere fun and different to take
the kiddies to.

Little Dudley House
77 South Street, Dorking,
Surrey RH4 2EU

www.littledudleyhouse.co.uk

A wonderful place for the whole family
to enjoy.

Dalmeny Hotel
19-33 South Promenade,
Lytham St. Annes, Lancashire FY8 1LX

Phone 01253 712236
info@dalmenyhotel.co.uk

A wonderful family hotel that Korin
visited on many occasions growing up
and still hold very fond memories of.

Lakeside Hotel
Lake Windermere, Newby Bridge,
Cumbria LA12 8AT

Phone 015395 30001
www.lakesidehotel.co.uk

For an escape to the beautiful Lakes
this blissful hotel offers both luxury
and serenity.

Drakes
43–44 Marine Parade
Brighton BN2 1PE

Phone 01273 696934
www.drakesofbrighton.com

A beautiful hotel in Brighton with a
2-red-rosette-star award restaurant.

**Radisson Edwardian Hotel
Manchester Opus One Restaurant**
'Free Trade Hall' Peter Street,
Manchester M2 5GP

Phone 0161 835 9929
resmanc@radisson.com
www.radissonedwardian.com/

Opus One is a great restaurant
attached to a great hotel. They open
for lunch and dinner and serve really
good British food in very chic
surroundings.

INDEX

How to Cook in High Heels

ThANKs

Well, what can we say, other than it's been such a pleasure! We hope you've enjoyed this book and that it's given you a true insight into our lives and has helped you see how what you thought to be impossible can actually be achieved. And, of course, we hope you've had some delicious results in the kitchen too.

We can truly say that we have had the best fun writing together. So now we would just like to say thank you to some of those who helped make this book possible – and our dream come true.

So, thank you to...

Jon Croft, our publisher at Absolute Press, whose witty sense of humour has given us the giggles on many occasions and whose insistence on champagne lunches has always been very much appreciated.

Matt Inwood, our art director, and fellow designer Claire Siggery whose joint creative flair has made this book look so delicious.

Meg Avent, our commissioning editor, who decided to take a chance on us (hopefully still no regrets!).

Laura James, our style editor, whose professional touch, knowledge and experience has made our book utterly fabulous.

Andrea O'Connor, our food editor, whose eye for detail picked up on our silly mistakes and ensured you've not been urged to make pizza for 500.

Mike Cooper, our photographer, and Genevieve Taylor, our food stylist – two very talented people who worked together to make the food look utterly amazing.

Victoria Kendrick, our beautiful make-up artist. Who needs airbrushing when we've got you!

Ailsa Macalister, our PR from Colbert and MacAlister, who ensured that we and our book are being seen and received so well by many of you wonderful people out there.

Fiona and Naomi at Kuoni for providing us with a fantastic prize for our readers.

And, of course, it goes without saying that without the endless babysitting duties from the grandparents, plus the essential guinea pig tasting, this book (and many of our other ambitions) would have been a lot harder to achieve. So a really big thanks to the following...

Our wonderful loving parents for all your support. To Julia and Bernie (Korin's mum and dad) and Pearl and Lenny (Sasha's mum and stepdad) – we love you all very much (and, yes, we can now pay you back all the money you've lent us over the years!). Liam, Bobbi and Eevy, our little angels, (not so little in your case, Liam). Words cannot describe how much we love you and thank you for being so patient with your mummies while we've been spending hours in the kitchen perfecting our recipes.

We've had our moments of tears, laughter and joy and this whole process so far has been a huge learning curve for both of us. But we realise just how lucky we are and don't take any of it for granted – after all, not many people get work with their best friend.

So finally we would like to thank each other for being tolerant, understanding and considerate of each other's needs and, well, just so bloody fantastic to be around all the time! Let's raise our Raspberry Belinis to many more wonderful years to come.

Sasha x
Korin x